STEVEN SPIELB

America Through the Lens

Martin Scorsese's America – Ellis Cashmore
Steven Spielberg's America – Frederick Wasser

STEVEN SPIELBERG'S AMERICA

FREDERICK WASSER

polity

First published in 2010 by Polity Press

Polity Press
65 Bridge Street
Cambridge CB2 1UR, UK

Polity Press
350 Main Street
Malden, MA 02148, USA

ISBN-13: 978-0-7456-4082-2
ISBN-13: 978-0-7456-4083-9 (paperback)

A catalogue record for this book is available from the British Library.

Typeset in 10.75 on 14 pt Adobe Janson
by Toppan Best-set Premedia Limited
Printed and bound in Great Britain by MPG Books Limted, Bodmin, Cornwall

For further information on Polity, visit our website: www.politybooks.com

TABLE OF CONTENTS

ACKNOWLEDGMENTS

Although this is a relatively short work, its genesis was encouraged by the enduring good will of many people. Andrea Drugan was a great mentor and editor, and the Polity staff have been very supportive. My approach to the topics was developed through discussions with Al Auster, Jakob Diel, Gerd Hallenberger, Peter Krämer, Angela Krewani, Paul Lopes, William Megalos, various members of NECS, Stephen Ogumah, and Karen Ritzenhoff. Jason MacDonald was a tireless researcher and helped immeasurably. Ann Klefstad guided my thinking and language at various stages. Dana Polan gave a generous and thoughtful response to some writing problems. The librarians at The Margaret Herrick Library, University of Southern California, and Emerson College helped to track down my eccentric requests. I received tangible support from the Research Foundation of PSC/ CUNY, the Provost of Brooklyn College, and the New Faculty Fund.

Nancy Berke provided essential intellectual support throughout the project.

The publishers would like to thank the following for permission to reproduce copyright material:

Page 3, 51, 68, 98, 134, 173, 177, 188 courtesy of Photofest; 44 © The Kobal Collection; 69, 201 courtesy of Herrick Library; 74 © Universal/ The Kobal Collection; 83 © Columbia/ The Kobal Collection; 106 © the United States National Archive; 140 © Tri-Star/ The Kobal Collection; 151 © Amblin/ Universal/ The Kobal Collection; 197 © Dreamworks/ The Kobal Collection; 209 © Dreamworks SKG/ Universal/ The Kobal Collection/ Ballard, Karen; 217 © Bettmann/ CORBIS.

INTRODUCTION:
CULTURE, POLITICS, FILM

American democracy has endured crisis and change in the last three decades. The second chapter in the postwar history of pop culture (which begins with the 1970s crises) has played out in dystopic ways: the global spread of American culture has coincided with declining interest and trust in civic life and public action in the United States and elsewhere.

Culture and politics reflect and determine each other in a relationship that has become increasingly perplexing. Right after World War Two, there was relative harmony between politics and culture in the United States. Within twenty years, however, this harmony was challenged by the rise of rebellious youth cultures. The ensuing turmoil and fervor led to the political exhaustion of the mid-1970s, which complicated the cultural situation for the members of the rising generation. The following decades were marked by political reaction. In the cultural sphere the rebellious generation of the 1960s had created new styles in film, music, and other arts. As the political reaction of the mid-1970s took hold, rebellion was rejected. Another style was synthesized, which emphasized direct personal excitement and sidestepped political conflict.

A primary manifestation of this exciting style is the Hollywood blockbuster; a central figure in the scenario of blockbuster evolution is Steven Spielberg. A creator of the contemporary blockbuster, he has managed to continue making such films through the decades, as American society embraced marketplace values that have increasingly polarized its politics. His big-budget films have reflected American society through this dysfunctional evolution and lately, contrary to the spirit of the 1980s, his films became increasingly historical and thus more political. This book will survey Spielberg's remarkable career as refracted through the prism of political shifts (both global and American) and as reflecting those shifts. The book has developed as an exercise in understanding the determining factors of Spielberg's career. The reader should know, however, that the inspiration for the book's title, *Steven Spielberg's America*, is America more than it is Steven Spielberg.

American culture is diffuse and impossible to know, while the career of one man is unified and knowable. The single career thus can serve as the visible marker of larger forces which are more difficult to track without such an index. This is particularly apt when the career is Spielberg's, because his filmmaking is in a profound relationship with large trends. He is very, very popular (he directed films that have earned $8.5 billion dollars at the box office and perhaps another $8 billion [and counting] in other markets). His films cannot be viewed as autonomous productions of a single artist but must be understood as industrial artifacts that have put together the largest audiences in the world. Always, they are expressions at some level of these audiences and their cultural-political situations.

It is received opinion that Spielberg shifted to more overtly socially engaged filmmaking after *Schindler's List* (1993). This shift correlates with erosion in US segment primacy in box-office support for the American film industry. Since that time non-US support has been a vital source of profits for Hollywood in general and particularly for Spielberg's politico-historical critical films. Spielberg has become the Hollywood director who both explains America to the world and gives the American perspective on world events. The global audience facilitates this role because they share with Spielberg a background in old Hollywood values. By recycling these values, his films shield themselves from the belligerent nihilism of other American blockbuster films. The conclusion—that loyalty to old Hollywood is not naïve, but overtly progressive—is one I find surprising in this age of polarized politics.

Spielberg at his favorite spot behind the camera on Close Encounters.

Steven Spielberg's America is an attempt to see how mainstream film handles the socio-political world. It is no longer
in question whether Spielberg's films are worthy; the worldwide audience long ago delivered that verdict. This book does
not attempt to uncover hidden meanings but to do something
just as difficult, which is to discuss meanings the filmmaker
negotiates with the audience. Spielberg constantly tries to
anticipate the audience, and in turn the audience turns to his
films to articulate aspirations and relieve anxieties. They
become the filmmakers. Walter Benjamin could have been
thinking of Spielberg when he wrote, "It is inherent in the
technique of the film as well as that of sports that everybody
who witnesses its accomplishments is somewhat of an expert"
(57). The young Spielberg wanted nothing more than to
share with the audience the thrills that he had envisioned and
constructed. This was the basis of his early success. The
resulting popularity guaranteed him autonomy to develop
himself much as a painter develops in a studio, with a certain
internal motivation towards evolving a critical realism. While
his films initially allowed the audience to smooth over political contradictions; now, in the post 9/11 world, a global
audience responds to his more critical view, although there
are always limits to his critical realisms. These limits are set
by his generation's insistence that public virtue can only be
judged by private happiness.

Spielberg's Generation and the Blockbuster

The trajectory of Spielberg's career takes the reader through
the three-way relationship between the contemporary blockbuster, the American political/social situation, and the historical turn in Spielberg. The filmmaker himself confesses to
holding both Democratic and Republican values. Without his

noticing it, his recycling of the "feel-good" spirit
lywood highlights the various stories' contradicti(
populism and private consumption. Populism,
movement to reform government and other puɒ... ...
tions so that public interests are paramount over market
forces, was a sentimental favorite of 1930s Hollywood. This
penchant occasionally tipped over into hostility towards
rampant capitalism. In the 1950s such populism was repressed
because of the general hysteria over the communist threat.
In the 1960s it appeared that a "New Hollywood" making
pictures of alienation such as *Bonnie and Clyde* (1967) would
revive populist themes as part of the civil rights movement
and countercultural protests over the Vietnam War. But this
was only a moment and soon faded.

Spielberg internalized both old and new Hollywood cycles
of populism and private satisfaction that characterize the
history of American filmmaking. His films gained prominence in part because they bridged these cycles and other
American contradictions, and as his career progressed his
work reflected an American ambivalence that is also increasingly an international one.

People wanted popular culture to do several things for
them: they wanted both excitement and reassurance. It therefore follows that political turmoil led to tumult in the American movie industry as well as in the culture generally. Several
movies of the 1960s had made themselves relevant to new
ways of thinking, but these films did not reassure the audience and so interest in such themes was not sustained. For
every isolated success within the genre of youthful alienation
were a couple of failures. The breakthrough came in the
1970s when Spielberg, George Lucas, and others were able
to achieve enduring success by developing stories with near-
universal appeal. Spielberg's narratives particularly favored
resolutions involving the restoration of the family as he

attempted to find motifs that would connect with the mass audience. Just as important as suitable stories, the popularity of these directors' blockbusters derived in large part from the construction and packaging of excitement that reached across the various political and cultural divisions in their audiences.

In hindsight this is not so surprising, since the supposedly progressive politics of that time had been ideologically ambivalent. Worldwide, the sixties signify a generation of young people losing faith in various governments and social traditions. While the counterculture of American youth initially had an affinity for the left, it turns out in hindsight that the loss of faith came from contradictory political traditions. The anti-establishment distrust of institutions reflected both left-wing disgust over government prolongation of colonial exploitation (Vietnam) and right-wing disdain for government redistribution policies (such as taxes and welfare). Spielberg, Lucas, and others (a shifting group that includes John Landis, Robert Zemeckis, and even older figures such as Richard Donner and more) pulled away from leftish stories of struggle and rebellion. But he and his colleagues did not revert to a right-wing Disney-like celebration of the American system. Instead they asked the audience to find satisfaction in private things, and they did so with a touch of youthfulness (and the mere hint of rebellion) that the older Hollywood had lost. In the felicitous expression of Peter Krämer, they made all-audience movies.

I will discuss the parallel development of Lucas and Spielberg in their finessing of the cultural divide. Yet even in these introductory remarks I should note that Spielberg sweated out the 1960s turmoil by directing episodic television for an elderly stay-at-home audience. Then he got out of television and used his first three breakthrough films to appeal to his fellow twenty-somethings. These were stories

of everyday men who are called upon to respond to the extraordinary. First it was David Mann outrunning and outwitting a demon truck in *Duel* (1971). Then Sheriff Brody hunted down a mammoth shark in *Jaws* (1975). In *Close Encounters of the Third Kind* (1977) it was Roy Neary deciding to seek out and board an alien spacecraft. While each had a flavor of new politics, in each case Spielberg relegated the politics to the background, in order to meet the primary aesthetic challenge of immersing his audience in the extraordinary; fear and thrill served that purpose in the two former cases and wonderment in the third. He was able to do so by means of an unprecedented skill in using the camera. He had solved the problem of compelling politically exhausted viewers to believe in the extraordinary existing in the ordinary.

THE IDEOLOGIES OF STYLE

Does camera movement have a political ideology? Spielberg's camera style was instantly acclaimed and accounts for his wunderkind success. Even his relatively obscure first theatrical film, *The Sugarland Express* (1974), caught the attention of America's foremost critic of the period; Pauline Kael, as well as the equally senior Dilys Powell of the London *Sunday Times*. It has been the least debated aspect of his talent, even though the contribution of such style to the socio-political meaning of the films is obscure and is entirely dependent on the context in which it is viewed. His camera style in *Duel* hooked a young adult movie-going audience even though the show starred Dennis Weaver, an older television star. Spielberg's camera blended television and cinema virtues and consequently brought together both audiences at a time when they were divided along generational lines. The camera moves to give the audience both an outsider's view and an insider's thrill. Spielberg does not hesitate to bathe the audience in light (see Chapter 3's discussion of "God Lights"); to shock them with dynamic edits; to startle them with the surround-sounds of the filmic events. Even though all of the individual techniques were already in use, it is their combination that amounts to something new—which scholars are starting to characterize as the blockbuster style.

The fast-moving, rollercoaster-riding camera and other techniques are means of manipulation, not of emotions, but of primal reactions. Jean Pierre Geuens breaks down stages of physical fright, from the immediate "flight or fight" reaction, to the emotion of fear, and then the response to and finally the reflection on that emotion (18–22). Movies have historically triggered secondary emotional reactions but now increasingly the techniques try to induce a primal visceral reaction in the audience, which is an immersion. Many critics distinguish blockbuster immersion from the classic filmic identification with the character by the viewer. Robert Blanchet writes of a "non-identificatory spectator address" where there is a "startle effect" that shocks the viewer in the audience even more than the character in the film (82–83). Spielberg is the primary practitioner of these effects.

This style did more than change the actual content of the movies; it also made them easier to market, particularly in the emerging multimedia markets of the 1980s and 1990s. Again Spielberg and his cohort had stumbled upon an attitude towards excitement that mirrored a speeded-up marketing cycle in American consumerism. It is integral to this innovative film style to enable more aggressive marketing techniques. The very word "blockbuster" was a huckster's term borrowed from World War Two pilots referring to bombs that could blow up entire city blocks. After the war Hollywood pundits used it to describe hugely successful movies such as *Quo Vadis* (1951), inspired by lines of movie patrons that stretched around the block. The filmmakers of *Jaws* and *Star Wars* (1977) developed the blockbuster style to launch a string of movies earning unprecedented amounts of money. They both caught and created a new wave of opportunities as movies were increasingly distributed on home video and found new audiences in foreign countries. By the end of the 1980s home video was contributing more money to Hollywood than the theatrical box office or any other single market. This money contributed to even bigger budgets and marketing campaigns. The home video success was not just a coincidence: the blockbusting filmmakers had grown up watching films on TV and almost unconsciously designed their films for both the big and small screens at the same time. The audience was quite willing to look at their films at theaters as well as on video cassette recorders (VCRs).

The first chapter of Spielberg's quest for all-audience appeal culminates with *E.T.* (1983). The second phase of the blockbuster begins when the pacing of films becomes quicker as the lessons of *Jaws*, *Star Wars* and *Raiders of the Lost Ark* were absorbed. (This is the overall argument of Shone, 2004.) The 1970s originators (notably Lucas) were left behind, leaving only Spielberg regularly directing new films. New directors—including James Cameron, Ridley Scott, Renny Harlin (in the 1980s), and Michael Bay (1990s)—evolved the big-budget action movies. But as their films conquered the box office, their slam-bang in-your-face style separated the all-audience out again. They were providing more exclusively masculine visual pleasures of destruction and mayhem. Spielberg's *Indiana Jones and the Temple of Doom* (1984) seemed to be part of this evolution.

But then Spielberg broke with the male-oriented trend. He left the action genre for five years to make more literary and historical films. When he returned it was with a kinder, gentler action hero. He continued to make thrillers and other high-stakes films but in contrast to the other dominant action directors, Spielberg was expanding his reach to a global all-age audience. As others' action heroes became increasingly nihilistic and isolated, Spielberg turned to stories about protagonists trying to enter a community. While his earlier films fitted in with Reagan's resurgent America, his films at the turn of the century had a more questioning relationship to the dominant political ideologies. Yet they still retained much of the blockbuster antireflective style. This retention of the style came from Spielberg's innate lifelong desire to please and was in tension with his mature ambition to engage hard questions. This tension paralleled America's own lack of political will to make hard choices.

CRITICAL REALISM?

Spielberg has made much of this post-*Temple of Doom* shift by explaining that he makes "serious" films alongside his "popcorn" movies. It is true that there is a distinct difference in earnings between the two sets of films but nonetheless the serious/popcorn distinction is misleading. All his films reflect the audience's desire. The audience wanted *Jaws* and *Close Encounters* to be escapist and so they were. The audience still desired wish fulfillment in *E.T., The Extra-Terrestrial* (1982) and it became a generation's cultural icon. Yet even in these "popcorn" films there was a portrait of a hollow America where public spaces had disappeared and loneliness predominates. Sheriff Brody (*Jaws*) faced a corrupt mayor and a megalomaniac shark hunter. Roy Neary (*Close Encounters*) had to turn to aliens for a sense of community. Elliott (*E.T.*) only got positive attention from his brother and the other kids when he became the alien's closest friend. The historic and political themes were present in the early Spielberg. He did not emphasize them since he knew that the audience used other parts of the filmic experience that he was offering them. In these earlier films the audience ignored the critical side of Spielberg's representation.

The audience ignored the less-than-rosy background of these films because of the relative benign turn of events for middle-class Americans in the 1980s. The threat of foreign powers was receding as totalitarianism began to run out of steam in the Eastern bloc and the post-colonial movement could not resist the global hegemony of market-driven capitalism. All around the edges situations deteriorated but the complacency of the affluent classes in the US and the West was not challenged and the reactionary politics of Reagan and Thatcher seemed to work. The long-term consequences of the gutting of labor and the stripping of public community could be ignored in popular culture.

As the audience becomes more international, however, and as consequences of the American Thermidorean reaction emerged in the mid-1980s, Spielberg pursues the genre of historical realism openly. He has the clout to draw attention to whatever kind of project he directs. Viewers follow him because they know that Spielberg will push the technology of moviemaking to give them a new experience—whether of historic realism or fantasy. *Schindler's List* (1993) and *Saving Private Ryan* (1998) reinvent the look of World War Two, while *Jurassic Park* (1993) pioneers new levels of computer graphics; levels that are pushed even further in *A.I.* (2001) and *War of the Worlds* (2005).

The historical film represents a shift in ambition. The initial ambition of the filmmaker was to please an audience by delivering entertainment: to gratify an audience with both experiences and emotions. The historical film invariably also has the political ambition of persuasion. This intimately ties the historical film to the documentary. The historical film uses history to speak of present times and to intervene

in contemporary politics.[1] One type of philosophical understanding is that all historical inquiries are attempts to understand the present. We shall look at the flexibility of Spielberg's
own representations of the past in many of his films and
uncover what current circumstances inspired him to make
such representations. Too many critics have been distracted
by *Schindler's List*, which is not Spielberg's great historical
film. It is not a film that makes a strong intervention in
current debates. Instead we should consider his subsequent
World War Two film *Saving Private Ryan*, the terrorist
thriller *Munich* (2005), and the science fiction *Minority Report*
(2002) as his true historical films, and even include *Catch
Me If You Can* (2002) and *The Terminal* (2004) as important
engagements with real social problems.

The blockbuster style, with its immersive techniques,
poses a philosophical problem when it is used in historical
films. The audience wants to believe in the reality of what is
being presented but if they are immersed in the reality by the
use of extreme techniques then they cannot step back to look
at the representation of history. Therefore the immersion
techniques altered in meaning as Spielberg started to develop
historical films in a later phase of his career. It is no longer
just innocent thrill-seeking fun. Sometimes his mastery at
making thrilling blockbusters leads to strategies in the
"serious" films that gloss over political contradictions.

Spielberg is in an intense mutual relationship with the
audience that is exemplary of popular culture. Therefore his
historical turn is fascinating. We are not used to a serious
turn among American filmmakers. It is much more a European tradition, and even in Europe it is a tradition that only
thrived in the lead-up to and aftermath of World War Two.
American filmmakers are very aware that their first obligation
is to entertain. Overtly political films have rarely commanded
the kind of box office that Hollywood expects. But the

historical film has been a genre in which, by tradition, politics and entertainment can be balanced for the mass audience. There is a continuous dialectic in such films between public spectacle and private romance (Grindon, 10–16). Historical fiction has the high ambition of presenting an entire world, ranging from the personal to the social.

Spielberg's best total picture of our current social problems is in *Minority Report*, released after the World Trade Center attack. While it is surprising that this science fiction has historical ambition, one philosopher of the postmodern, Fredric Jameson, has speculated that science fiction is the film genre that supplants the historical film. His speculation anticipates the achievement of *Minority Report*. The two earlier Spielberg science fictions—*Close Encounters* and *E.T.*— delighted the audience with the wonder of the universe, and had less regard for current social engagement. Much later his science fiction *A.I.* pivoted away from feel-good entertainment, and more recently *Minority Report* and *War of the Worlds* turned 180 degrees away from delight, in order to contemplate democratic society's response to destruction. I will argue that we should look at a string of movies—from *Saving Private Ryan* to *Munich* seven years and six films later— as a continuous engagement that staged the contradictions of those moments. The fact that the audience came along for such a change provokes my inquiry into the parallel changes in the filmic and political spheres.

I am struck that Spielberg's imagination always wanted to wander over the past but that the "new world" circumstances of sunbelt culture suppressed historical understanding. Spielberg's imagination comes from the movies. By this time movies represent a legacy, an accumulation of a generation of sound films with an even longer backlog of silent-era movies. This archive of films exerted its influence, and was actually able to preserve earlier attitudes and belief systems, even as the world moved on to new ways of doing and seeing. In this way movies represent an alternative to the monolith of present-day culture. A postwar generation used movies to escape the confines of the era's circumstances. The new waves of cineastes from France, Italy, and Great Britain specifically looked to older films as well as films from other countries to give them a perspective on their own lives. Spielberg was the American who also looked to the movies for his political and cultural education. At least one critic has noticed that while the French filmmaker Jean Luc Godard and Spielberg cannot be further apart in earning power and aesthetic ambition, they share a love of cinema (see Hampton). In both cases this love reinforces their politics. In Godard's case the politics are radical, in Spielberg's the politics are consensual liberalism.

These politics are informed by old Hollywood and help to separate Spielberg from current filmic nihilism. His touchstone is "classic A-listed Hollywood adventure movies." He listed *The Treasure of Sierra Madre* (1948), *The Adventures of Don Juan* (1949), *Only Angels Have Wings* (1939), and *Casablanca* (1942) as influences on the "Raiders" series (Freer, 97). This is the bond he has with the audience even as American politics drifted rightward away from the humanism expressed in *Sierra Madre* and *Casablanca*. He has the magical ability to remind his audiences how much they love those movies. He is constantly reminding his actors that they have felt this emotion before by conjuring up the image or scene from their collective celluloid memory. By extension this is what he is doing with his viewers, and part of that collective memory is the populist sentiments of prewar Hollywood. As audience shifted overseas, he discovered an ever-widening circle of shared celluloid memories, some of which even include his own earlier films.

From the beginning, Spielberg retold classic Hollywood stories of adventure, the wrong man accused, romance and chicanery. But as the American political system started to show strain in subsequent decades as the result of the systematic erosion of public institutions in the 1980s, his stories took on a more realist tone and assumed the historical film's ambition to address current politics. Is it just the contrast between the populism built into these stories as they were first filmed by the likes of Alfred Hitchcock, John Huston, and Frank Capra and the current political reaction that gives *Minority Report*, *Catch Me if You Can* (2002) and *The Terminal* (2004) a decidedly political edge? Is Spielberg overtly preaching politics in his less-acclaimed "pedantic" pieces such as *Amistad* and *Munich*? The answer is yes to both.

A partial explanation of the historical turn is a desire to see if the verities of Hollywood still hold up. This much Spielberg can get the audience to agree to. It is a relatively safe approach since (just as in populist old Hollywood) his stories rarely encourage us to question the entire premise of our current system. They play at socially satirizing consumer society but will not attack consumers. They critique the simulacra of reality and yet use the latest in computer graphic technology to replicate reality. They become unwitting allegories for a society that always hopes there is a way to avoid tragedy, to not make hard choices. In short the stories have limitations and contradictions that illuminate larger shortcomings. If we look at his entire career, we can see the cultural status of liberal political belief systems in the mass audience. This is an achievement in itself; it reveals the global existence of an audience that had learned its liberalism from Hollywood. The Spielberg movies served as an important sign of alternatives within the American mainstream, when there were few such signs.

Future Itinerary: Where Did He Come From?

This book places Spielberg into several contexts. One over-arching context is the socio-political world, and the other more local one is the film industry, generally American but increasingly global as his career progresses. While discussion is organized around each of his films, the goal is to elucidate the situation of the audience, the film world, and that historical moment. I begin with the foundations of Spielberg's imagination: the postwar sunbelt, Hollywood and early television, the new emphasis on private life and the family. But when Spielberg becomes old enough to go to Los Angeles, his formative experience is his generation's counterculture, inspired by disdain for the Vietnam War to seek out and create alternative media. He witnesses the rise of New Hollywood while he gets a job directing television episodes. He is assimilating these influences when he gets to make a feature film. He thus picks a story of youthful alienation, just as that "New Hollywood" theme is fading. The subsequent disappointment motivates him to drop the themes of New Hollywood and to develop a blockbuster formula that results in the break-out success of *Jaws* in 1975.

That success and the box office explosion of movies such as *Star Wars* (1977), *Raiders of the Lost Ark* (1981), and others are analyzed in the next section. During the Reagan years, popular culture is being reshaped and Spielberg is at the center of this reshaping. The cultural mood is hardening and Spielberg initially goes along with this hardening when he makes *Temple of Doom* (1984).

The second half of the book examines Spielberg's growing interest in historical realism. He explores a separate way, diverging from other action directors, subsequent to *Temple of Doom*, and the question becomes: is the audience following him, or does he abandon his explorations in order to regain a mass audience? This consideration takes us to the *anno mirabilis* of 1993, with the releases of *Jurassic Park* and *Schindler's List*. Here Spielberg pulls off the feat of two very successful films, rather neatly divided into "popcorn" entertainment and serious, engaged historical film. This is all too neat. *Schindler's List* does not solve the issue of whether a blockbuster filmmaker using cinematic techniques for visual excitement can engage in critical realism.

The next decade brings new challenges for this kind of filmmaking with the increasing importance of the global audience and political challenges to the role of government. *Saving Private Ryan* (1998) actually engages these contemporary problems but its visceral style tends to paper over the contradiction in the story between private happiness and public duty. Spielberg returns to the same types of realism in *Catch Me If You Can* (2002) and *The Terminal* (2004). But a more successful critical realism is to be found in *Minority Report* (2002), which is an entry in the emerging genre of digital apocalypse. These chapters bring the reader up to the current changing global situation and the filmmaker's continuing relationship with a changing audience as he continues a series of remarkable films.

1

THE FORMATION OF
SPIELBERG'S GENERATION

It is fruitful to interpret the well-known Steven Spielberg biography as the formation of both a filmmaker and the primary member of the first generation to experience film on television. He was born on December 18, 1946 in Cincinnati, Ohio. His father and mother were of Jewish descent. During his childhood, observation of the rituals and laws was relaxed, yet Steven knew he was different from the Protestants who typically were his neighbors and classmates throughout his youth. There were soon two younger sisters who completed the family. The Spielberg family left their aunts and uncles in Cincinnati, and were on their own when they moved to New Jersey in 1949. The family moved again in 1957 to a development outside Phoenix, Arizona.

SUNBELT CULTURE

Phoenix and the surrounding parts of Arizona were booming in the 1950s as part of a new region in the United States called the sunbelt. The swath of land below the 37th parallel stretching from Florida to southern California acquired this name after the term "sunshine belt" was first devised by Air Force pilots (Goldfield, 3). In World War Two America projected its power across both the Atlantic and Pacific for the first time. This involved the deployment of many Eastern men to the Western states where these men experienced open country and year-round sunny weather.

California's rapid postwar growth spilled over to other sunbelt states. The widespread distribution of the newly invented air conditioner and the postwar national commitment to building an interstate highway system opened up additional parts of the Southwest, particularly Arizona. The sunbelt soon acquired several positive connotations. The housing stock was new, with many amenities targeted at the middle class. Contractors took advantage of the open spaces and built units rapidly for single-family house owners. The economy would be based on service and high-tech industries.

Spielberg's father, Arnold, was one of those World War Two soldiers who had been deployed to the Pacific front from the Midwest, and now was one of many veterans moving their families to the West. He was following a pioneering national migration; in addition, his career was emblematic of the postwar economy since he was adapting his electrical engineering skill to the new field of computer electronics.

In New Jersey, young Steven first experienced the movies and television. The family bought a Dumont TV set in 1949 (Champlin, 12). He seemed very sensitive to the emotions that were conveyed by movies and television and his parents curtailed his viewing of these media to some extent. In Arizona he took charge of the family's 8mm camera and that led to his lifelong fascination with visual storytelling. The boy had full access to the popular culture of his day and

correspondingly did not show much interest in books. Spielberg claims Arizona as his true boyhood home although the
family relocated for a final time to California in 1964, while
he was in high school. Arizona was where he developed a
mania for movies and started making them with his pals. His
biographers can just about trace all of his later movies to
obsessions he developed at this point. These include he and
his friends acting out scenes of combat that referred to the
recent war, watching shooting stars in the night sky, watching
TV, and even the trauma of living through a family estrange-
ment and the breakup of his parents' marriage.

That the adult Steven Spielberg claims Arizona as the
region central to his formation is important. Regionalism has
contributed less and less to our understanding of American
culture during the course of the twentieth century, since mass
culture is centrally produced and distributed on a global basis.
This is unfortunate. Regionalism is still a strong cultural
marker, but it has to be understood in ways that are not based
on simple linear geography. The sunbelt has become the
landscape of aspiration for the affluent inward-looking self-
contained American family. The suburban mindset has risen
to permanent dominance across the political spectrum. This
attitude naturalizes the desire to center life on private domestic matters while viewing public institutions as (un)necessary
evils. It took a while to incubate in the immediate postwar
period until these sunbelt values became manifest in the
politics of the 1970s.

Many contemporaries were wary of emerging suburbia.
Lewis Mumford wrote in 1961, "This was not merely a child-
centered environment: it was based on a childish view of the
world, in which reality was sacrificed to the pleasure princi-
ple" (Mumford, 494). His sour words were about suburbia in
general but highlighted the dangers of sunbelt culture. The
sunbelt accelerated the centrifugal force of suburban culture.

Unlike east coast suburbs, the sunbelt developments no longer looked to an urban center for their cultural life. The new lifestyle created a demand for an even more efficient technology of cultural distribution, which undermined the need for proximity to heterogeneous centers. Television was one such distribution technology, and it could deliver both picture and sound to the isolated houses of the desert sprawls. Already, Mumford could write that children do not see "the workaday world; plac[ing] an undue burden of education on the school and family ... reality has been progressively reduced to what filters through the screen of the television set" (496).

While watching television did not trigger great intellectual aspirations, it was what Steven had. Growing up in the sunbelt's tabula rasa, the television became his window on the world, his guide to the past. The housing was built overnight invariably on recently subdivided pastures and fields. There was little sense of history clinging to the terrain. The postwar migrants did not even have their own rooted connections to other parts of the country since they were, themselves, a generation removed from the land or the product of earlier migrations from Europe who had few personal links to American history. They could only see the land as a given.

Television did little to help white Americans understand the lands of Arizona and California. Early TV westerns ignored or whitewashed the removal of native Americans and Spanish-speaking settlers while concocting a new myth of the redeemed Southerner conquering the West for the benefit of all. This mythification was as egregious as other myths of origins ranging from Virgil's *Aeneid* to *La Chanson de Roland*. Its obvious falsities would become apparent (at least to historians) as the 1960s civil rights movement forced a more honest look at nineteenth-century American history than American television was able to portray (see Nadel, 2005).

The myths of the West discouraged an interest in historical culture among the new inhabitants of the sunbelt, and at least one boy seemed frustrated by the discouragement. One senses when reading the oft-told recollections of the young Steven getting an 8mm camera and filming his friends acting as soldiers, cowboys, or space invaders, that here was someone whose imagination wanted to engage the history of the Arizona landscape, but did not have the native stories with which to do it. Spielberg's potential for a historical imagination had to make do with the spatially remote events of World War Two, for lack of visible evidence of the temporally distant repressed events that still cling to the Arizona or California land. He would later turn to the topic of lost histories and buried bodies in suburban landscapes in collaboration with his fellow sunbelter Tobe Hooper in *Poltergeist* (1982).

THE FAMILY'S INFLUENCE

Suburbanization is a spatial manifestation of a cultural shift towards family-centered life and consumerism. As this shift occurred people tended not to think of themselves as carpenter, engineer, or clerk but as "regular middle-class folks." They were moving away from a production-oriented identity to a consumption-based identity. "Middle class" became a very flexible term adopted by just about everyone, and it came to include a wide range of incomes and education levels. The unifying center of the middle-class identity was no longer work, but a family lifestyle based on high levels of comfort and consumption.

The production/consumption shift undermined notions of public life and enhanced the status of family-oriented living. This was a change from an earlier stage of American democracy that was founded by people who applauded public life.

"Enlightenment thought [eighteenth century] . . . held that public values . . . were qualitatively different from and superior to private values of love and personal nurturance" (Coontz, 1992, 96). The long nineteenth- and twentieth-century turn towards the private was intimately tied to mass media growth. Magazines, films, and eventually broadcasting all promoted a leisured life centered on the domestic hearth as a refuge from the public world of work and commerce. This kind of attitude became the basis for the American longing for the suburbs, which were removed both from industrial work in the town and from agricultural work in the countryside.

No cultural movement is monolithic and linear, however. Even the relatively unified group of films being produced by the major Hollywood studios would cycle through different messages and different ideologies, though always within a mainstream consensus. For example, in the 1930s Hollywood occasionally glorified public action and told populist stories of work and workers (see Lary May for an extended argument of this thesis). This was a time when unions and the labor movement strove for the dignity of workers and legislation was passed to give unions some rights. But in the 1950s anticommunist hysteria did much to undermine people's belief in either workplace solidarity or collective action. Two sets of values competed, and on television Steven Spielberg could watch the populist 1930s movies, while in the theater the current Hollywood movies would reflect a backward movement towards private domestic stories.

Postwar media insisted in a thousand daily messages that marriage was the source of life's satisfactions. The extended family of grandparents, uncles, aunts, nephews and nieces loses status and economic/emotional functions while the tight group of husband/wife/children increases in emotional importance. This also made the emphasis on family life more important as an alternative to fracturing communities. "The insistence that marriage and parenthood could satisfy all an individual's needs reached a peak in the cult of togetherness among middle class suburban Americans in the 1950s" (Coontz, 2006).

Spielberg's parents divorced in 1966 when he was nineteen but the marriage was apparently troubled long before. This colored his childhood. In the larger society divorce was becoming common, perhaps unsurprisingly. The pressure on contemporary marriage was intense precisely because the relation had become so important. The suburban family had only themselves for companionship. It became a facet of American life that other relationships were subordinated to the primary relationship of marriage. Spielberg's generation continued to accept the intensity of marriage and, currently, are not surprised when it spills over into the public world of politics or even international relations. Americans want family-type feelings from their stories, their movies, and even their political leaders.

The postwar period had some notable public-sphere successes. The G.I. Bill helped Spielberg's father and millions of others to receive higher education. Other social networks had been put in place by the federal government. These, however, fell far short of similar networks being constructed by European countries. In 1948 President Truman desegregated the United States military. There was a growing affluence and a feel of triumph after the victory of World War Two. Americans took pride in setting into motion the successful Marshall Plan that helped rebuild the economy of Western Europe. The civil rights movement was growing and drawing sustained momentum from global anticolonialist politics. But there was also the stalemate of the Korean War and concern over the expansion of communism and the Soviet development of the atomic bomb. The fear of

communism facilitated a backlash against the labor movement. It also seemed to be the background for a high
degree of conformity in everyday life. The mood of the
nation was hard to generalize. Ambivalence between public
activities and private contentment played out in the formation of TV.

TELEVISION AND DISNEY
IN THE SUBURBS

This generation was the first to experience television as a
formative medium; it was becoming the source of tradition
in the new suburbs. Its programming was distributed from
coast to coast by the three networks: CBS, NBC, and ABC.
In the first few years programming was diverse; there were
anthologies of live dramas featuring many different settings
and experimental news documentaries. It stabilized in the
later 1950s, around a predictable roster of nightly news
reports, wholesome situation comedies and cheaply made
episodic series restricted to three or four genres (predomi-
nantly Westerns). This nationally disseminated content
solidified the postwar feeling of a unified nation that had not
been prevalent in the prewar, more regionalized, United
States.

At first the center of the TV world was New York City.
New York continued to host the corporate headquarters of
TV broadcasters, but after 1955 the production center rapidly
became Los Angeles. Television production moved to Los
Angeles to take advantage of the expertise and efficiencies of
film production studios already located in southern California. New York also had some unfortunate associations that
advertisers wanted to avoid, such as left-wing politics and
ethnic exoticism. California seemed more "white bread" and
wholesome. TV took advantage of the Hollywood industry's

established relationship with the American mainstream. A hybrid version of the sunbelt attitude started to permeate television.

But television's relationship with the film industry was not straightforward. The attempts of the Hollywood studios to take powerful positions within broadcasting largely failed due to a variety of factors. There was hostility from government and advertisers, and there was the lack of investment money. Thus a natural convergence was postponed for more than three decades. Nonetheless the children in Spielberg's generation were heavily exposed to the Hollywood products featured on primetime TV. Studios such as Warner Brothers and Universal started making the routine westerns and police shows that filled out the broadcasters' programming. A minor Hollywood studio, Disney, used its television show to promote both its films and its new theme park, Disneyland, and eventually became the biggest cultural provider of the twentieth century. And slowly television opened up Hollywood's archives.

The obstacle to showing movies on TV through its first decade was that the broadcast networks were unwilling to pay what studios thought films' exhibition rights were worth. So the only movies that were available on television in the early 1950s were the occasional Hollywood exceptions such as *The Wizard of Oz* (1939), which CBS paid a huge sum for, and movies from foreign and bankrupt studios such as Arthur Rank and RKO, since these companies were quite willing to take what little they could get. Generally such sales were made to independent stations looking for non-network programming. The irony is that foreign films (mostly British) were more available on early TV than they have been since, because of such cheap sales. Yet foreign films on television were presented to the viewers as if there was nothing special about them. TV famously deprives stories and images of their context and the casual viewer might not even notice that a film was from another country. The medium juxtaposes all levels of genre and production into an endless flow of images and talk. The films on TV had to fit into the rigid schedules of the stations, which typically broke down the hours into fifteen- and thirty-minute sections. They also had to be interrupted for commercial advertising breaks. This early generation thus had an eclectic education in film culture as they grew up on television.

Although Steven Spielberg complained in later years that his parents closely monitored his TV viewing, he seemed to watch many popular shows designed for his age group, particularly *Disneyland* (ABC 1954–1961, NBC 1961–1981, a.k.a. *The Wonderful World of Disney*) and *The Mickey Mouse Club* (ABC 1955–1959) (McBride, 62–64). He and the rest of his age group received heavy exposure to the "Disney version." Disney's influence on moviemakers of Spielberg's age was a more conservative force than the other Hollywood movies starting to appear on television.

The Walt Disney Company helped fashion a turning point in postwar American culture. The company opened the Disneyland theme park in 1956, in Anaheim, California, approximately a thirty-minute drive from Los Angeles and in the heart of the territory occupied by the expanding aerospace industry. Disney had famously financed the park's construction by making a deal to provide child-oriented programming to the ABC broadcast network. This provided an opportunity for aggressive cross-media marketing using the TV show to promote both the park and the film releases. Disney's strategy became the forerunner of the cross-media marketing of the modern blockbuster. The TV show, films, and park rides were all used to promote the sale of related merchandise, cartoon books, and music records. The ubiquity of Disney in 1950s culture made it hard to remember that the studio was only a minor player in prewar Hollywood. Disney became the face of suburban culture, with a decidedly sunbelt complexion.

The company helped create sunbelt culture but it was not of it. The Disney artists had rural, urban and European backgrounds. Disney's own American upbringing had brought him through a variety of circumstances—he had lived in the city, a small town, and on a farm, struggling in all of them. The stories he and his workers had used in the 1930s for their shorts were mildly populist, puncturing big business and rich-folk sensibilities. For the feature-length animations, Disney turned to stories that had connotations of the European courtly and high-art traditions. This is true of *Snow White and the Seven Dwarfs* (1937), *Pinocchio* (1940) and *Fantasia* (1941). Both the cartoons and feature-length animations won wide admiration for their artistry and inventiveness. Walt Disney's own vision was somewhat technical, but his studio won artistic prestige. Schickel reports that Disney himself was pleased with the admiration of intellectuals and other critics, although he did not fully understand it (Schickel, 208).

Both the embrace of European traditions and the populism changed during the war and its aftermath. Walt Disney himself became bitter after a fierce strike by workers at his company in 1941. He was thoroughly anti-communist in his beliefs, and his company dropped any critical themes and became pro-corporate in their scripts. Their productions turned mostly to American themes and, in particular, to historical treatments of pioneering days. *Davy Crockett* and *The Swamp Fox* portrayed the American fight for "freedom." The Disney portrayal admitted no warts and eliminated any suggestion of slavery or even racial prejudice. Texas John Slaughter and Zorro were deliberate attempts to give an American history to the sunbelt. Zorro was a unique treatment of the Hispanic chapter of California history. Yet such multicultural diversity was diluted by a complete elision of class conflict: a hero of the upper class was shown fighting for the benefit of all. It flattered east-coast viewers by completely paralleling the conflict between California creoles and Spanish authorities with the thirteen colonies' struggle against Great Britain.

Disney's turn to history was part of the studio's embrace of American triumphalism during the Cold War. This reactionary gave a new generation a whitewashed version of America that was more demagogic than textbooks if only because it was on TV. Even a biased political print source has to acknowledge complexities of the American story that a TV adventure series can blithely ignore. Disney cold-war ideology dropped the "older, optimistic, inclusive populism of the Depression era" (Watts, 288) and now espoused "a notion that the nuclear family, with its attendant rituals of marriage, parenthood, emotional and spiritual instruction, and consumption, was the centerpiece of the American way of life" (Watts, 326). The inward-looking Disney doctrine would permeate Spielberg's work and create a bond with his audiences.

SOCIAL CHANGES AND THE AMERICAN FILM INDUSTRY

Suburbanization and consumerism led to a lifestyle change that emphasized using weekends for recreation and enjoying new experiences. Its rise is measured in the increased expenditures that Americans made on golf, tennis, and other equipment-driven recreations. These leisure alternatives destabilized the movie industry and declining attendance forced the industry to respond. Darryl Zanuck, the head of Twentieth Century Fox, wrote memos about this shift to participatory leisure in 1953; and he astutely decided to use

Cinerama, CinemaScope and other wide-angle film formats
to make movie going more of a participatory event, compared
to previous films or to television (Belton, 77). The black-and-
white, grainy television image was relatively unexciting. The
movie industry saw an opportunity. It revived long-dormant
technologies to make the movies a big theatrical experience.
More films were made in color, and budgets were bigger than
before.

Spielberg reports that Cecil B. DeMille's *The Greatest
Show on Earth* (1952) was the first movie that he saw in the
theater. At that time, he could not have been aware that he
was witnessing one of the movies that started the "road show"
period,[2] which ran from 1952 until 1966. The films of this
period were spectacular, often using wide angles, always
bigger than life, and certainly bigger than television. In addition, the plotlines favored international locales and often
were set in the past. These movies could make a lot of money.
In 1956, *The Ten Commandments* had a domestic gross of $86
million. This sounded hopeful for a teetering film industry
but the studios could not generate enough hits. Nothing
came close to surpassing *The Ten Commandments* until a
decade later with *The Sound of Music* and its gross of $160
million. The road show was a high-stakes gamble and many
studios actually posted annual losses, something they had not
suffered even in the lowest point of the Depression.

By 1965, the year of *The Sound of Music*, both visual media—
television and movies—felt out-of-touch to an increasingly
politicized youth culture. Earlier, American leadership had,
largely successfully, negotiated the expansion of government
benefits on the domestic scene and the containment of communism through the Cold War and the post-colonial reshaping of the world. Few questioned mass media's conformity
and celebration of the political mainstream. The turbulence
of the 1960s exposed the shortcomings of this political

leadership, however. American foreign policy lost direction in the quagmire of Southeast Asia, while the civil rights movement was undermined by summer riots in the inner parts of American cities. Segments of the global media audience started to peel away from the mainstream culture, which was not yet ready to question the direction of the country.

In the two decades following the end of the war there was a growing American subgrouping based not on regional difference but on age. The grouping developed a small but influential counterculture that expressed itself primarily through music. As radio lost its national audience to television, the individual radio stations played more local music. This helped young people to discover "authentic" folk music or avant-garde jazz that could form a counterweight to the oppressive top-down centralized production of television and film. The people who participated in this kind of exploration of music were also interested in images and storytelling. Comic books and underground films provided something of a visual outlet for this emerging generational culture. This segmentation was also occurring overseas, particularly in Western Europe. Youth culture exploded across different media in London, in fashion, in photography, in hairdressing, and in music in the early sixties. Big movies and television were not initially important to the formation and expression of this culture. Youth culture was an afterthought in the movie box office. Nonetheless, it was an afterthought that led to a sea change in Hollywood. What resulted is now termed "New Hollywood."

New Hollywood was both a change in the content of the films and a change in who was making them. An older generation of producers and directors who had dominated movies since the introduction of sound was now moving on. In the 1950s road show era, the old filmmakers were still working. John Ford (1894–1973), Alfred Hitchcock (1899–1980),

Howard Hawks (1896–1977) are a few examples who were making their most remarkable films at the end of their careers (Krämer, 2005, 81–87). They had first learned their craft in the old silent-era studio system. One of Spielberg's favorite road show epic directors was David Lean (1908–1991) who came up in a similar way (albeit a generation later in England). It was natural that after forty years of sound films a new generation of filmmakers would be forming. The question was, where they would be recruited from?

The end of the studio system after the Paramount *et alia* consent decree of 1948 eroded a natural in-house apprenticeship program. Yet there were new possibilities for apprentice filmmakers in the development of television and the introduction of lighter and cheaper equipment. Television production was initially headquartered in New York City and borrowed talent heavily from the New York theater. Unproved talent who had some minimal exposure to the equipment from their military service could apply. Thus we have the beginnings of the careers of Robert Altman (1925–2006), Sidney Lumet (born 1924), and Arthur Penn (born 1922), all of whom worked in TV and then switched to feature filmmaking. Penn went on to direct *Bonnie and Clyde*. Mike Nichols (born 1931) came in from theater and directed *The Graduate*. The dual release of these two films in 1967 launched New Hollywood.

For this cohort, television training was what theatrical training was to the first generations of film directors. Much of the aesthetic of early television concerned its difference from film. In this rhetoric, TV executives emphasized that TV was live, often making a virtue out of a necessary limitation. Thus Lumet and Penn cut their teeth in live television, with its emphasis on acting and staging and its relative lack of art direction or other refinements of the image. Intensity of emotional acting was enhanced by its immediacy through

live transmission and was valued over the beauty or excitement that could come from visual imagery. The TV image
was low in resolution, high in contrast and zero in color.
Broadcasting a prerecorded film also worsened the quality of
the original photographic image. Generally, television directors decided it was the medium of the close-up, because the
image was so small and degraded. This emphasized the actor
and reinforced the theatrical milieu of TV. Even when television production moved to Los Angeles and was taken over
by film veterans, the close-up and a relatively static camera
continued. This was the fastest way to shoot and TV shows
were always shot on vastly abbreviated schedules compared
to film. There was no time to move the camera or to go out
on location.

The antecedents of New Hollywood were not just in early
television but also in the "B" movie market of the 1960s. In
this decade there were fewer movies being made by the major
studios and the existing theaters suffered from not having
enough films. They were desperate to show anything they
could get their hands on. A genre of "exploitation" films was
developed by new companies such as American International
Pictures (AIP) to feed this theatrical hunger. These movies
were made very cheaply with subject matter that attracted
young people: often "teenagers in trouble" stories. Teens
now expected a commercial culture that specifically targeted
their generation. Drive-in movie theaters played these low-
budget movies designed for a young audience. The production values were low-scale while the topics were more salacious
than was considered possible on television. Foreign films also
helped fill the product-starved theaters and were quite different from television. Several new distributors, based in New
York, brought in European films. Many of them did quite
well because they had adult themes, and went further in
exploring sexual material than any American producer would

dare. Foreign films increasingly won a significant share of the
US box office. Beginning in 1958 and continuing until 1968
there were more foreign films in US theaters than domestic
ones (Steinberg). Even though the majority of imports were
not high earners, foreigners took home more than 10 percent
of the US market in 1959, 1960, and 1961 (Lev, 15).

AUTEURISM AND NEW HOLLYWOOD

The combination of foreign films in the downtown theaters
and television in the living room led American critics to
reexamine high and low art. Television was mixing all the
levels of art together while the foreign film had pretensions
of high art that American films had not claimed. These
imports tried to reflect the personal concerns of the filmmakers to a degree that fascinated American critics. The
foreign directors were used to claiming validity for their films
as personal statements, as opposed to commercial vehicles.
To be sure, the most profitable imports, such as *A Man and
A Woman* (France, 1966), had commercial aspirations, but
the overall rhetoric of foreign films was one of artistic
autonomy.

In 1954 Francoise Truffaut, working as a French film
critic, coined the term "la politique des auteurs" to motivate
an examination of whether a body of work by a film director
had the same aesthetic cohesion as the oeuvres of acclaimed
novelists or painters. This act of criticism was applied to
Hollywood filmmakers as well as foreign ones. He and other
critics argued that Hollywood filmmakers operating within
the studio system were capable of great personal expression
within the generic and other formulaic restraints of the
industry. Thus even American filmmakers could be creating
high art. When Truffaut made his criticism, it was purely ex
post facto descriptive. But then two things happened. He and

his French colleagues started making films and embodied in their own work the aspirations of an "auteur." Furthermore, in 1962 Andrew Sarris popularized the auteur theory in the United States. Now even Hollywood studio filmmakers wanted to act as "auteurs." They wanted to tell stories as personal expression as opposed to merely telling the most popular stories.

The auteur theory was of a piece with the rising influence of the counterculture. The counterculture despised industrial production of culture and espoused self-expression. It had a romantic notion that economic success should only be the result of the people's embrace of the artist's authenticity. This was a source of debate in music as rock stars started to earn astronomical sums and their organic connection with a community became questionable. The audience's desire for authenticity amplified the influence of auteurism in the film industry. It was inevitable that auteurism became a marketing device for various films. For example, the American trailer for Antonioni's 1966 *Blow Up* tried to sell the American audience on the virtue of "Antonioni's camera." More movies were introduced to the audience with the credit of "A film by [director's name]". The director became known to more moviegoers than before. The auteur theory was taught in the various film schools that were expanding during the 1960s.

At the same time, the counterculture movement started to develop a more complicated relationship with Hollywood than simply ignoring it. Some popular filmmakers wanted to assert their auteur ambitions and their countercultural bona fides in the mid-1960s. This came to fruition when two important studios released *The Graduate* (Embassy) and the very edgy *Bonnie and Clyde* (Warners) in 1967. Immediately the critic Pauline Kael championed *Bonnie and Clyde* as a breakthrough; in hindsight, both of these films crystallized a new audience of people tired of the commercial mainstream.

The episodic structure of *Bonnie and Clyde* undermined the classic style of old Hollywood, and its ultra-violent ending was enabled by the recent dismantling of the Production Code. *The Graduate* was less provocative, but decisively different from old Hollywood romances. The adulteress did not suffer and the leading man was not very heroic or even sympathetic. This was the beginning of "New Hollywood," in which the heroic motivation was less obvious and the endings were more ambiguous than in classic Hollywood.

The new sensibility was successfully designed to attract younger viewers to mainstream theatrical films. These new kinds of films co-existed with the other genres, but a trend had been established that moved away from the road show epics. The big money-making movies between 1952 and 1966 were romantic and skewed towards female tastes. As New Hollywood began to set the trend, historical films disappeared, fewer films were shot at international locations, and male stars predominated over female leads. Even big-budget romances were targeting the adult female audience less frequently at the end of the decade than at the beginning.

Individually, many of the new Hollywood directors had sympathies with left-wing politics, but their stories tended to focus on the psychology of their protagonists rather than the politics of the situation. Hardly any movies openly espoused political rebellion or offered critiques of consumer capitalism. The more successful ones, such as *Midnight Cowboy* (1969) and *Easy Rider* (1969), had the flavor of disdaining the establishment while making politics a matter of lifestyle, not public action. *M*A*S*H* and *Catch-22* (both 1970) more directly criticized US military institutions, albeit not the actual policies of the current government. Hollywood (new and old) notoriously avoided the Vietnam controversy. Psychological foci fitted the more muffled approach to political themes in Hollywood that was the long-term consequence of the 1950s blacklistings. For a few years in the late 1960s, cultural activity was also political expression. The mass audience could visibly flirt with rebellion by flocking to movies about new ideas and buying records of psychedelic music.

The conflation of politics with cultural rebellion was exemplified by *Easy Rider* and its appropriation of music. Rock music had attracted a large mass audience. Much of rock music had roots in the folk music movement of the 1950s, and continued the folk tradition of expressing political passions of the times. Filmmakers, interested in the music and the politics, became interested in the new music audience. They successfully tapped into this audience with the 1969 release of *Easy Rider*. It was made for $340,000 and earned rentals of $19.1 million, and was one of the top earners for its year.

Easy Rider took New Hollywood in the direction of youth films made by relatively young people. The door was finally opened to film school graduates by some young relatives of old Hollywood. Bert Schneider (born 1933) was the son of a former president of Columbia Pictures. His partner Bob Rafelson (b.1933) also had prominent show business relatives. They teamed with Henry Fonda's son, Peter Fonda (b.1940), and his partner, Dennis Hopper (b.1936), to make *Easy Rider* in 1968 for a July 1969 release. Fonda and Hopper were veterans of the exploitation circuit, as was their third co-star, Jack Nicholson. Although there was some Columbia money behind the film, it was made very cheaply using classic exploitation techniques. But the enhanced distribution power of Columbia gave the film huge profits and all of Hollywood took notice. The film strongly targeted the youth movement, featuring drugs, rock 'n' roll, and the motorcycling lifestyle. The lesson learned, or so the studios thought, was to turn the studio keys over to younger filmmakers. Such youngsters were easily recruited from film schools. Francis Ford Coppola,

George Lucas, John Milius, and many others became part of the first wave of the film school generation to have careers in New Hollywood.

POSTWAR CULTURE FRACTURES

American postwar culture was a decisive change from the years of economic depression and world war. But the postwar desire for stability was already falling apart by the time of Spielberg's maturity. The drive for change was not due to the outside pressures of the Cold War but was instead fed by internal contradictions and shortcomings. By 1969/1970 the political-cultural fault lines were evident. The first chapter of the postwar era had come to an end. Culturally the division was running along generational lines. But socially and politically there were other fractures. A more visible fracture was between the races and a more ubiquitous one was between men and women. A somewhat submerged one was the erosion of the consensus between organized labor and capital. It was not at all clear how these social tensions would play out.

Steven Spielberg came of age at the confluence of these years. He was not going to be an actual rebel or experimenter. But he had paid attention and would assimilate the audience's conflicted desires to be hip and inclusive of the new movements, and to turn away from the exhausting political conflicts. His attitudes were formed by growing up in the most representative sector of the emerging new culture. His sense of politics and of history had been shaped by growing up in the new space of the Arizona sunbelt. His eye and imagination had been shaped by the formative medium of TV. As we will see in the next chapter, television had as many things to teach him as a director as it had taught him as a TV viewer.

2

SPIELBERG GETS HIS BREAK

A key factor in discussions of Spielberg's career and its context is always his birthdate. Those born around 1946 were separated decisively from those who came before. They were able to take advantage of unique opportunities that would no longer be available to those who came after. His generation craved a more exciting visual narrative. As George Lucas explained in 1997: "Steven [Spielberg] and I come from the visceral generation. . . . We enjoyed the emotional highs we got from movies and realized that you could crank up the adrenaline to a level way beyond what people were doing" (Shone, 12). When the "visceral generation" came of age they sought compensation for the visual deprivation of early television. Within imposed limits, Spielberg learned how to crank up the excitement on television and thereby earned a chance to make theatrical movies. He and Lucas concurrently started to make movies that appealed to this visceral long and added in other filmic pleasures to evolve a film styl would bring in an "all-age" audience in the late 1970

SPIELBERG GETS A JOB

The path to filmmaking for Spielberg was going to be through television directing. Starting in 1962, he showed the determination to go further than other aspiring teenagers by making his pilgrimages to the Los Angeles film stages. He famously used the Universal tour of their stages to get off the beaten track and wander around on his own to meet the still-working legends of the time. Alfred Hitchcock had him thrown off the set and John Ford gave him some obscure advice on where to frame the horizon in a shot. Despite these inauspicious meetings, he was learning to admire the directors rather than be distracted by the stars. He continued these practices and actually became friends with Chuck Silvers, an editor on the Universal lot. This and other friendships he established during this era were later of great use to the young man. He managed to graduate from high school and to begin his studies at California State College at Long Beach in 1965. His enrollment was motivated in part by the college deferments that protected students from the Vietnam-era draft at that time.

But his real focus was on making films. Even the regular filmmaking classes at Long Beach were not allowed to get in the way. He teamed up with some well-financed wannabes who produced his showpiece short film in 1968. The result was *Amblin'*, which was shot on professional 35mm film. It is a poetic tale of a college-aged youth meeting a free-spirited young woman as they hitchhike through the California landscape. They share life together for a day and a night and then separate casually with only a slight wistfulness. The film caught a mutual attraction between the hippie girl and not-so-hip boy. *Amblin'* was a pitch-perfect expression of the attraction of the free life for the boy, who nevertheless rejects it the morning after.

This flirting with a freer way of living was characteristic of its director, who would only flirt. He did not embrace an alternate path. As a child Spielberg only heard whispers, on television, of an American avant garde existing in big cities on either coast. Later he had more access to such rumbles of nonconformity through his interest in comic books—in particular, *Mad Magazine*. He didn't show much interest in San Francisco's literati, however, even as his family moved to the area. He did share the anti-establishment antipathy to the Vietnam War that was growing by the mid-sixties.

Spielberg did not want to be an outsider even at the opening of his career. He did not pursue the grass-roots method for distribution that other filmmakers were exploring in order to be independent of the major studios. He deferred such efforts to his partners who were trying to get *Amblin'* into theaters. Instead, he used the film as a calling card for his entry into the studios. He got to show it to a top executive based on his friendship with the editor Charles Silvers. Impressed by the movie's fresh visual imagination, Universal's number two man Sidney Sheinberg soon offered Spielberg a directing contract. All of a sudden, Spielberg was no longer on the outside. He was now in the mainstream and he was going to direct TV episodes, at the tender age of 22, for Universal Pictures.

UNIVERSAL TV: MOVIES ON TELEVISION

Universal was physically one of the oldest studios: Carl Laemmle built it in Universal City, California, in 1912. In the late 1960s it was moving towards a movie/television convergence. MCA had risen to power doing a lot of agency business in broadcasting in the 1940s and 1950s. It finally acquired Universal Pictures in 1962 to form the first conglomerate in Hollywood. Its CEO, Lew Wasserman, moved energetically into many different aspects of show business, including reviving Universal's now-famous studio tour in 1964. Television production was the steady source of profits through the decade, even as the studio upgraded the film division by signing big stars and directors. But the television side had more of the flavor of old Hollywood, since it had a large staff who had begun their careers in prewar movie studios and were now working steadily cranking out episodic dramas.

Universal's signing of the young man was a half-step sooner than everybody else in town. Within two years the other major studios would bring in young people to make films, in the wake of *Easy Rider*. It is unclear whether Sheinberg had the same motivation to "get young," or whether he was just objectively impressed with the talent he observed on the screen. Nonetheless, a forward-thinking executive may well have anticipated that it would be smart to have a young director on the staff as television programmers increasingly sought the same young audience that film was discovering. The 1968 prime-time season had *Rowan and Martin's Laugh-In* (NBC 1968–1973), *The Smothers Brothers Comedy Hour* (CBS 1967–1969), and *The Mod Squad* (ABC 1968–1973). These shows were all attempting to attract a young audience that had largely abandoned television. Universal had yet to break into such youth-oriented programming. In addition, Universal made theatrical films, and may well have hoped that a 22-year-old could help there. That was for the future; more immediately Sheinberg started his new hire in the form of television that most closely resembled film: episodic drama.

Spielberg's first Universal assignment was a segment of a television pilot for *The Night Gallery*. The segment was called "Eyes" (NBC aired it November 8, 1969) and it was written by television's most famous writer, Rod Serling, who was already winding down his career. There was no thought that Spielberg would slant the show towards a young audience. He was just there to cut his teeth as a journeyman director. Although he chronologically belonged with the film-school generation, he was going to be anointed with the luster of the old studio system. The great movie star Joan Crawford was the lead for the episode. While Spielberg was still feeling the full flow of gratitude for getting a directing contract at a studio, his ambition was to direct theatrical films, and he considered television directing a chore. The 22-year-old man had the painful task of trying to establish authority over a veteran Universal crew with credits going back to the golden years of film. Nonetheless, he was lucky to be in the right place, at the right time, receiving precisely the right training. There was a loose fit between the director and the crew, since the young man was largely self-educated and did not have film school baggage. Other young directors were making their mark with student films (Lucas) or scriptwriting (Coppola, Milius) and were generally not apprenticing under the old hands. This was in contrast to Spielberg who was forced to work with an older production staff to attract a mature audience.

"Eyes" was a tense shoot and did not lead immediately to another assignment. Spielberg took advantage of his position, however, and the slack time between his first and subsequent assignments, to watch movies and to socialize with the film-school crowd of his own generation at USC and elsewhere around Los Angeles. We can assume that he filled out his knowledge of European and other ambitious films at this point, since he had not systematically studied film history (American Film Institute).

Towards the end of 1970 and through 1971 Spielberg's career picked up and he moved through a string of directing jobs, including the first regular episode of *Columbo* as it began

*The young director working with Crawford and other
Hollywood veterans.*

a series run on NBC. These assignments did not give him an
opportunity to seek out the youth audience that was now the
obsession of the theatrical film industry. Universal TV projects continued to rely on a middle-aged audience. Television
notoriously erases traces of the director's personality because

the director typically has to shoot quickly, working with a producer, crew, and cast who know the show much better. Even today, it is not a director's medium. But Sheinberg had some sympathy for his wunderkind and was adroit at giving the newcomer TV assignments that developed his imagination. Anthology shows like *Night Gallery*, or episodic television such as *Columbo*, were the TV genres that provided opportunities for a visual director. For example, in *Columbo* there was only one continuing character. The villain and all the other characters could be molded by the director. The complete cycle of the story from beginning to end was completed in one episode. The sets were new and different from other episodes. The style was generally single-camera and the shooting schedules were a little longer than other TV shows. A shrewd director could do something.

It was a sign of his genius that Spielberg did manage to assert a stylistic consistency across the various TV episodes he directed. By instinct, he negotiated two goals that were in tension with each other. The first was to stand out, the second was to show competency. He anticipated that unique visualization would win a ticket to filmmaking. Part of the reason that the "Eyes" shoot was a stumble was that his attempt to stand out with a series of bravura shots gave the episode a reputation for being out of balance and too arty. Thus he had to rebalance and give greater emphasis to the craft, as it was defined by old Hollywood, which was typically the classic style of overly obvious melodramatic realism. As he learned to balance, he acquired the career-long habit of remaining true to the old craft while continually finding fresh ways to establish a distinct look.

The older generation of the industry had seen TV as less than the big-screen film, and avoided wider shots since they did not believe that the added visual detail would give much to the home viewer. The producers claimed the added time to get visual enhancements was wasted on the small screen. The TV close-up gives intimacy to the small screen in situations ranging from the news anchor talking directly to the viewers to the domestic plotlines of soap operas. The close-up was even prevalent in action genres such as Westerns and detective stories. Some have argued that it is precisely television's limitations as a visual medium that motivates more "technical events" such as zooms and the appearance of words on the screen (Mander, 303).

By the late 1960s, however, those limitations were less severe. There had been enough investment in better equipment at both the transmission and receiving ends for TV to approximate some of the visual pleasures of the big screen. Spielberg literally got to reevaluate the visual power of television. We remember that he had his formative audio-visual education from TV. Even though he was loyal to big-screen films, he had developed this allegiance by watching them on the small screen. His work instinctively took advantage of TV's incremental improvements, and he was not going to discount what he could do visually in the medium. He worked against small-screen prejudices by cutting down on the number of close-ups, favoring the high angle wide shot and moving the camera. He claimed in later interviews that he was allowing the audience to edit their own shots by giving them multi-character wide shots from which they could pick the characters they wished to watch. This was film-school talk, however, that should not be taken at face value. He was as interested as any filmmaker in directing (and manipulating) the viewer's attention.

TV producers did not oppose Spielberg's camera movement but challenged him to do it on a tight schedule. He responded by extensive pre-planning (honed by his childhood filming) to meet the challenge. Camera movement has accrued different meanings over the history of cinema. The montage school of filmmaking avoided camera movement because it was distorting, and undermined the power of frame composition (Harrah, 170). It drew too much attention to the camera itself, breaking the illusion that the audience is seeing reality itself. Thus in Hollywood there developed the distinction between motivated and unmotivated movement. If the camera followed the action (motivated) then it did not break the illusion. Unmotivated camera (such as the camera dancing around two seated men talking) might break the illusion and was to be used only in heightened moments of drama. But the fear of breaking the illusion lessened as the audience became more familiar with cinema. Indeed, television had immersed everyone, including the stay-at-homes, deep in cinematic language all the time. Visual directors were starting to lose their timidity after sixty years of cinema history. Experimenters had already decided to edit shots together without regard to classic style. Spielberg was merely one of the first "non-arty" directors to assume that even the middle-brow TV audience "stays with the story" when presented with attention-getting camera movements.

As the reasons discouraging camera movement faded (people saw that the audience didn't get distracted, the illusion of realism was not compromised), reasons for movement become compelling. Camera movement is an easy way to show cinematic sophistication. Amateur filmmakers do not have access to wonderful props, beautiful locations, exquisite lighting, glamorous stars, or even competent actors. Amateur 8mm camera production teaches them to seek excitement in ways that will play despite the lack of production values. With a little practice they learn to move the camera steadily to add excitement. Now these home movie amateurs were moving into the studio system to become directors. Spielberg was the first to be so picked and the first to tease out the new capabilities of the audience.

Spielberg goes very far with this new faith in the television audience in his direction of the *Columbo* script entitled "Murder by the Book" (NBC, aired September 15, 1971). Since he uses this show to get his big breakthrough assignment on *Duel*, it is instructive to see how far he goes. He begins with an overview of light traffic on a Los Angeles side street and the incongruous sound of a typewriter, and then has an unmotivated pullback to reveal a writer typing in a high-rise office by a picture window overlooking the LA suburban sprawl. There is a cut to a framed magazine cover photo of two writers receiving an award, and again a pullback to a frontal shot of the writer. This play between outside and inside is justified, as the viewers find out that the plot hinges on the murderer enticing the victim out of the city to a lakeside resort. The writer is killed up there. A second murder also occurs in this isolated resort while the investigation and the arrest take place back in Los Angeles. Although the script and the characters had already been developed before the director was hired, it was the director who managed to emphasize a relationship with the landscape. Spielberg uses the moving camera and the wide shots to show us the living conditions of the sunbelt, pleasant in details, monotonous against the horizon, hiding murderous impulses underneath bland smiles.

The *Columbo* episode was a success and launched one of the more popular TV shows of the decade. Meanwhile, Spielberg saw another way to pursue the sunbelt theme when he read a Richard Matheson short story called "Duel" in *Playboy* magazine about a mysterious truck harassing a lone motorist on the empty byways of Southern California. Matheson was already a famous science fiction and TV writer. His stories used the austere conditions and heightened anxieties of the desert to portray universal conflicts (see Riordan). Spielberg immediately saw the nature-versus-man aspect of "Duel" and knew it was the perfect showcase for his visual abilities. He was chafing to get out of television and into feature films. There was some talk of making the story into a regular movie but ultimately the studio executives decided to make it into a relatively new format: a TV movie. Spielberg was making his transition via this hybrid.

At the end of the 1960s Universal aggressively pursued TV movie production and entered into a relationship with ABC to make such movies. The decade had shown that home-bound Americans were still in love with the movies; it was just that they no longer wanted to go to the theaters to see them. The highest-rated TV shows were the various movies shown during prime time, such as *The Bridge On the River Kwai* (ABC, aired September 25, 1966). The movies were so popular that within a few years networks were running out of their library leases on the old films, and the studios were correspondingly charging more for recent films. Universal sold Barry Diller of the ABC broadcasting network on the idea that making their own movies directly for TV would cost less than leasing Hollywood movies, and would still attract the movie audience and earn commensurate ratings. No one really had a formula for making such TV movies. In those first few years it was still a genre in flux.[3]

Spielberg took advantage of this relatively open new genre to propose making a movie without dialogue. This proposal came out of his eagerness to stand out and do something with towering ambition. Ultimately the movie had some dialogue, but his vision of a taut minimal movie was strong enough to make *Duel* (ABC, aired November 13, 1971) one of America's unique TV moments.

The opening sequence sets up the triumph of the sunbelt sprawl over the traditional city as the car leaves the crowded streets of Los Angeles. Spielberg places the camera in front of the car to give the car's point of view (not the driver's) to make sure that we the viewers are leaving the city along with the protagonist. It is a bravura series of lap-dissolved shots strung together for about three minutes that was actually added later, after the main body of the film was completed. Spielberg knows what he wants to tell us and is not going to be timid about pulling us into the landscape. The continuity of the shot is very faithful to the actual geography of Los Angeles as the car swings out on the Pasadena Freeway and then merges with the major interstate heading north. Finally clear of the city limits, Spielberg cuts to an external view of the car driving on the open roads of Los Angeles County 30 to 40 miles north of the city. The actual setting was on California Highway 14. A generation earlier this land was only for livestock, occasional farms, and oil drilling. Only now in the late 1960s did it become at all plausible to portray a salesman driving these roads to get to a business meeting. *Duel's* hero, the businessman David Mann, played by Dennis Weaver, is a pioneer, still somewhat out of place. His isolation intensifies when a truck aggressively overtakes him and then tricks him into the passing lane precisely when an oncoming car makes passing impossible. Mann is forced into a skid but regains control. The duel is on. We will never learn who the truck driver is or why the truck wants to crush the protagonist. Mr. Mann finally outmaneuvers it and tricks the truck into driving itself over the cliff, as the prey outwits the predator. It is the return of the sunbelt man to raw nature.

Screen direction was all-important to the duel. Spielberg maintained an overall logic of left to right in the opening sequence, but knew he must vary the direction. He was not rigidly tied down, in other words he did not lose his audience for the sake of a formula. He softened the changes with bridge shots, and camera movement across the rear of the car and the truck. At this point he switched to a dominant pattern of right to left with masterly pacing and cutting to convey story points in a very austere drama of car versus truck. There were uses of new wave techniques such as deep focus and allowing the lens to flare (Buckland, 81–83). These flourishes were a soft bending of the proverbial Hollywood rule book.

In another matter Spielberg won an outright fight against the studio rules. The production manager Wallace Worsley said that the production schedule could only be met if process shots were used. This was a cheap way of managing car shots by filming the driver in the car in the studio while the passing landscape was either projected on a screen behind the car or added later in optical printing. Spielberg insisted that he was going to shoot the actual car being driven in the actual location. He won this fight and thereby highlighted his commitment to *not* ask the audience to believe in the make-believe of a studio shot but to *live* the experience of actually being in the hostile location as the truck tries to destroy the man.

Dennis Weaver in Duel.

The paring away of distracting elements and the reality of the locations had the effect of forcing the audience into intense identification with Mann. There is very little relief from his point of view; the audience gets no more information than he does. Even inside a multi-character roadside café scene, the camera stays with Mann. Famously, Mann and the audience never find out who the truck driver was nor the motivation for the pursuit. Spielberg never asked the viewer to become interested in David Mann as a three-dimensional human being. Instead of thinking about the story, the audience felt the adrenaline rush of his situation as the truck sped up from the rear or tried to run Mann over as he placed a phone call.

Duel drew a respectable television audience. More important, there was an excited reception within critical circles and the suites of the TV/film industry. Cinema International Corporation, a cartel of Hollywood distributors handling the international market, decided to release the TV show as a theatrical film overseas. The foreign release was a success. Spielberg was sent on his first overseas trip. The young man from the sunbelt had only a few ideas about the world that he had gotten from television and movies. He sought out and had a nice meeting with Federico Fellini, the great Italian film director. But his first encounter with Italian critics was an exercise in miscommunication. Spielberg reported later that "I had four critics in Rome walk out on a press conference when I refused to say this picture [*Duel*] was really the battle between the upper classes and the working classes in America today" (American Film Institute, 34).

But Spielberg's provincial American rejection of a European political analysis was a knee-jerk response, not the finished position of a mature artist. He was not overtly political as the term was understood at the time, but he was sympathetic to the various movements and later expressed regret over his first film's (*Amblin'*) lack of commitment to the politics of the day. He was nothing if not a quick learner, and an extended Spielberg quote from 1978 shows that he had been silently influenced by the Italian critics' questions. It demonstrates that he was fully capable of his own bitter class-oriented interpretation of *Duel*.

> *It begins on Sunday; you take your car to be washed. You have to drive it but it's only a block away. And as the car's being washed, you go next door with the kids and buy them ice cream at the Dairy Queen and then you have lunch at the plastic McDonald's with seven zillion hamburgers sold. And then you go off to the games room and you play the quarter games Tank and The Pong and Flim-Flam. And by that time you go back and your car's all dry and ready to go and you get into the car and drive to the Magic Mountain plastic amusement park and you spend the day eating junk food.*
>
> *Afterwards you drive home, stopping at all the red lights, and the wife is waiting with dinner on. And you have instant potatoes and eggs without cholesterol—because they're artificial—and you set down and turn on the television set, which has become the reality as opposed to the fantasy this man has lived with that entire day. And you watch the prime time which is pabulum and nothing more than watching a night light. And you see the news at the end of that, which you don't want to listen to because it doesn't conform to the reality you've just been through prime time with. And at the end of all that you go to sleep and you dream about making enough money to support weekend America. This is the kind of man portrayed in* Duel. *(Baxter, 77)*

Spielberg was playing with this negative view of suburbia after he was caught off guard by a Marxist view of his film. Was he describing a man trapped or a man who has embraced his limited fate? It seemed to be a lament for the former.

While Spielberg the political thinker would continue to be confused among a variety of libertarian and socially conscious impulses, Spielberg the storyteller emerged from television with a sincere interest in the lifestyles of his presumed audience. He wanted to tell stories in which ordinary people can prevail, and their motives are worthy and do not need to be critiqued. It was a classic position inherited from old Hollywood and was in contrast to New Hollywood's explorations of ambiguous protagonists being crushed by an anti-human system. But this period's Spielberg is not completely explained by old Hollywood's Pollyannaism. He identified with his own generation and their "rejection" of conformity, and eventually he developed stories where his dual loyalties to both worthiness and nonconformity could be reconciled; in 1975 with the sheriff who defies the political leadership in *Jaws*; in 1977 with the suburban man who willingly goes off into space in *Close Encounters of the Third Kind*. But when he got his first theatrical film in 1972 his instinct was not fully formed. He needed to learn from the rest of Hollywood.

Searching for Balance After New Hollywood

By 1972 (and with the benefit of hindsight) the critic can establish that the initial phase of New Hollywood, which explored rebellious deviant psychologies from Clyde Barrow in *Bonnie and Clyde* to Ratso and Buck in the Oscar-winning *Midnight Cowboy* (1969), had run its course. *Easy Rider* was now also some years in the past and the attempts to launch an entire slate of counterculture films at mainstream studios had resulted in fizzles such as *Alice's Restaurant* (1969) and *The Strawberry Statement* (1970). The protests against Vietnam were fading as Nixon started to seriously draw down the American forces after his re-election. The civil rights movement had also lost some of its high drama, due to a backlash and to the ambivalence of fighting for changes when the barriers were more subtle than legal segregation. But the trauma of American politics continued into the mid-1970s as the malfeasance of the Nixon administration was exposed in 1974 in the cluster of corruption known as the Watergate scandals. These scandals had the power to outrage fellow politicians, the media, and the electorate.

The major studios would finance a properly framed anti-establishment movie script if executives anticipated an audience. But no one was sure of what the frame should be. There are three examples of films that constructed a new frame and therefore pointed to a post-New Hollywood synthesis. In 1969, Paramount bought the best-selling novel by Mario Puzo called *The Godfather* and eventually approached a film-school generation director, Francis Ford Coppola, to make the film. He was not attracted to the genre of Mafioso gangsters until he talked himself into thinking that the movie could be a critical overview of a corrupt American society. He talked Marlon Brando and other actors known for their intensity into sharing his vision. When the marketing department saw the soon-to-be-completed movie they were enthused and decided not to showcase it but to go into the relatively wide release of 323 screens by its second week in March 1972. The result was a huge moneymaker (the North American box office took in $135 million in its first release) that attracted an audience with its glamorous portrayal of ruthless power. Because of the glamour it is not clear whether the movie really conveyed Coppola's hostility to American corruption to its audiences.

In 1970 Warner Brothers agreed to produce a mixed bag of vigilantism and alternative New Age philosophy called *Billy Jack*. Here again the studio and the filmmaker had two different views of the frame. Warner Brothers thought the movie was a small martial arts film. Their marketing and the resulting box office was mediocre. Tom Laughlin had produced, directed, and starred in the movie. He believed in the story as a strong political and cultural statement. He was angry enough at Warners' marketing to sue the company. The result was that he bought the film and re-released it using innovative local TV advertising and a town-to-town campaign in 1973 that eventually returned $32 million. His ability to do this on his own drew the industry's attention, particularly to his use of local TV spots. Television advertising by the major studios went up 80 percent in 1974 (Wasser, 1995, 57). These episodes proved that the old genre expectations were breaking up and that there were audiences for various political and cultural messages. Overly overt political messages did not seem to work, but genre benders such as glamorous gangsters and a sincere New-Age warrior could appeal to very profitable audiences. It was up to the filmmaker to figure out how to appeal to these audiences and how to get them into theaters through the marketing of the film on television.

Coppola's protégé George Lucas wanted to make a film based on his own teen years in the town of Modesto, California. The location would place the story in a sunbelt town, which allowed Lucas to ignore the problems of racial diversity, and the era depicted in the film assured the audience of innocence, before the trauma of Vietnam. Nonetheless the loose narrative of unfocused boys and girls on the verge of graduating high school and exploring their sexuality and need for autonomy had some critical overtones reminiscent of the James Dean classic *Rebel Without a Cause* (1955). Executives at Universal, relying on the perception that youth films had run their cycle after the demise of *Easy Rider* imitators, were very reluctant. Coppola had enough clout to make the project go ahead and Lucas got to direct what became *American Graffiti*. It was released in the summer of 1973 and became a big hit (domestic gross of $115 million). The nostalgia of Lucas's story attracted those who wanted to escape politics while the music and the teenage setting brought in those who identify with rock 'n' roll. Lucas had stumbled across a way to attract a wide audience interested in teenage lifestyles but wary of rebellion and dramas of alienation. His synthesis had surprised movie executives.

THE FIRST MOVIE: *SUGARLAND*

After *Duel* Spielberg went on to make a few more TV episodes but everyone knew his future was in directing feature films for theatrical release. The question was which film to make. This game was already in full progress by the mid-1970s and the young tyro devoted himself to it. He had the extreme confidence to reject scripts while waiting for the right one. For example, he turned down *White Lightning* (1973) and the chance to work with Burt Reynolds because he anticipated that it was not the right first film. With choice comes responsibility. Spielberg already faced some of the artistic problems of his generation. His choice of a project would be a statement from him about who his audience was, and for whom he wanted to tell stories.

In 1973 Spielberg committed to his first theatrical film: *The Sugarland Express*. The story came from a true incident in the newspaper. He teamed up with two of Lucas's USC classmates, Hal Barwood and Matthew Robbins, to write the script. The extended car chase aspect of the story seemed tailored to the director who had made *Duel* and the powerful producing team of Zanuck and Brown decided to

make the movie for Universal Pictures. It was released in
March 1974.

The story is about Lou Jean Poplin (Goldie Hawn) who
has had her baby taken away from her by the State of Texas.
She forces her husband Clovis (William Atherton) to escape
from a minimum security prison just weeks before his sched-
uled release in order to get the baby back from the foster
parents. She again forces him to kidnap a policeman (Michael
Sacks) at gunpoint and all three start driving towards the
foster parents' town in the police car. The state police, led
by Captain Tanner (Ben Johnson), pursue them, but at a
distance, since Clovis is threatening to kill the policeman.
The chase becomes a media event and many along the side
of the road cheer the fugitive couple while various hotshots
join the chase in order to hunt the bad guys. Captain Tanner
tries to manage the hotshots, the enthusiastic crowds, and the
kidnappers themselves. The chase comes to a bad end when
Clovis is shot dead by sharpshooters from the Texas Rangers.
The policeman is freed and Lou Jean is imprisoned, although
a final title card tells us that the real Ms. Poplin is eventually
reunited with her son.

The choice of the film material suggested that Spielberg
was still fascinated by New Hollywood's stories of rebellion
and had not thought to adopt the safer balance of themes of
American Graffiti. Not just Spielberg but various filmmakers
at this time thought that the audience might want to see
young people doomed by the law. Terence Malick's *Badlands*
(1973) and Altman's *Thieves Like Us* (1974) preceded *Sugarland* by only a few months. Spielberg may have regretted that
three titles split the potential audience, but even in aggregate
the business for the three movies did not suggest that the
mass audience was interested any longer in outlaw lovers.
The era that was launched by *Bonnie and Clyde* was coming
to an end.

The tragic ending of this film had a great resonance with the earlier tragedy, but there were key differences. The focus of audience identification was off. The Poplins were not as involving as the Barrows, since the audience quickly recognized their incompetence and saw them as inferiors, not as flawed heroes. The anger and the violence were less extreme. Spielberg became divided in his own loyalties. As a member of the younger generation, the filmmaker was curiously sympathetic to Captain Tanner, who was portrayed as the reasonable man caught in the middle. Neither Malick nor Altman had similar sympathies for the chasers of their doomed couples. This sympathy was a surprising instance of Spielberg's sincere love of his characters—*all* of his characters. Pauline Kael's review of *Sugarland* at the time mentioned this trait of the rising young filmmaker and she favorably compared his warmth with the coldness of the other young riser, Terence Malick (1974).

Malick also followed a true story, but one that was twenty years old. Spielberg could actually be less contrived and more mobile with his camera because his setting was the near present. The long sweeping car chase once again gave wings to his camera. He used the rolling hills of Texas to show cars stacked one against the other from one crest to the next crest. He set the chase in the fast-fading world of country roads, paying no attention to the Interstate highways. It is interesting to watch this movie several decades after it was made. There were no global fast food outlets like McDonalds or Burger King. It was rural America still untouched by big-box stores such as Wal-Mart. Still, the movie's honesty about its setting suggests that these transformations were about to happen. Fast food and trading stamps did exist. Lou Jean was fascinated by consumer catalogs and mass-produced merchandise. It was a world on the verge of omnipresent consumerism. Simply by placing the camera in contemporary

Texas, Spielberg, with more intuition than analysis, glimpsed the soon-to-be future of rural Texas. He even conveyed a fast-disappearing culture of work. While some characters made reference to their backgrounds as farmers, the movie avoided the actual site of legitimate work and labor. The only labor shown was a metal scavenger picking through an abandoned car. At this time the American labor movement was in the midst of a steady decline. It had lost its socialist zeal during the anti-communist years and subsequently had not managed to be relevant to either the civil rights or anti-Vietnam war movements. But the loss of working-class prestige had not attracted much film-school generation attention and *Sugarland* only alluded to this loss.

Spielberg was not of the rural heartland although his own suburban background in Arizona gave him some proximate knowledge of Texas. The casting of Ben Johnson as Captain Tanner worked from this perspective. Johnson was strongly associated with the Western, particularly those of John Ford. He had always played the quiet competent sidekick. He did not have the swagger of John Wayne or Charlton Heston and therefore was acceptable to a youthful audience who would have resented those other towering monuments of patriarchy. Peter Bogdanovich had already established this soft persona for Ben Johnson three years previously in *The Last Picture Show*. Therefore Spielberg intuited that the audience would identify with the lawman who was in the middle between the forces of rebellion (the Poplins) and the forces of right-wing nihilism (the vigilantes and other hotshots).

The Sugarland Express did not go as far as *American Graffiti* in uniting youthful characters with safe appealing themes. In the future, genre blending would be a key ingredient in Spielberg's construction of a blockbuster audience.

Therefore *The Sugarland Express* is interesting precisely because it points the way towards genre blending, but its mixture of tones resulted in cognitive dissonance for its audience. Goldie Hawn had previously played in comedies, and her active albeit unwitting role in the shooting death of her husband confused and upset the audience. The moviemakers were stumbling upon a problem that Michael Ryan and Douglas Kellner described as an "exhaustion of genres" in the 1970s. The storytellers were not fully invested in either tragedy or triumphant heroism. But the lesson was not to abandon their ambivalence but to rebalance it in favor of heroism. For Spielberg this meant a further interest in the middle figure; the everyman as the hero. Clovis Poplin could not have been the hero; he was only the middle ground between Lou Jean and the kidnapped policeman. The audience's middle ground was between the privacy of the couple trying to reclaim their baby and the vigilantes out to kill them in the public square. Those were the possibilities in the early 1970s. Spielberg said after making the movie that he should have built up Captain Tanner for the audience to identify with. In his next film, a sheriff was the everyman hero in the middle.

On the Cusp of the Blockbuster

When the task is to anticipate the audience, the mass media artist has an advantage over the social analyst. The analyst would have seen American society polarized and unwilling to compromise. President Nixon was being consumed by the Watergate scandal because of his highhandedness both in ordering subordinates to conduct illegal activities against his enemies and in refusing to release evidence. This highhandedness was the culmination of decades of anti-communist hysteria that had led Nixon to the White House and over the brink of paranoia. The analyst would have thought that the absurdities of Altman's *Nashville* (1975) or the double crosses of Coppola's *The Conversation* (1974) reflected the times. But Lucas and Spielberg had started to sense a void, and they anticipated that the large audience wanted the older movie virtues again, but with the full adrenaline ride. Spielberg moved away from the grit of *Sugarland* to give the American audience the cranked-up ride of *Jaws*, while Lucas started scripting the mythic universe of *Star Wars*. As Lucas said above, they wanted to attract the visceral generation.

Directors born in the 1940s seemed to have an instinct that their audience would accept a further push, one that would expand the limits of cinematic language. Pauline Kael described having a drink in 1976 with an unnamed director of the older generation who said of Spielberg, "He must have never seen a play; he's the first one of us who doesn't think in terms of the proscenium arch. With him, there's nothing but the camera lens" (1976, 136). The older director was noticing the development of the immersive style, a style committed to getting the audience to experience the full dimensionality of the action. Mander, Bernardoni, Eidsvik, and most recently Geoff King trace TV's impact on movie style in camera movement, technical events (such as zooming), and kinetic editing.

The road show movie style was premised on doing exactly what television could not do. It held wide landscapes and huge crowd scenes for lengths of time, to allow the audience to revel in the photographic detail of the spectacular. These huge wide shots would fall apart or otherwise be boring on the small screen where the photographic detail could not be seen. A young director could anticipate that the audience wanted spectacle even on the small screen. Therefore the directors who came up in the seventies worked on a style that was not in opposition to the television, but instead would convey a visual energy that would play in any format. This is a movie style that does not use the space of the big screen to do more than is possible on the small screen, but that plays with vigor both on television and on film, often with a hand-held or otherwise very kinetic camera movement.

Spielberg had developed a high-energy style in television, mostly by trying to immerse the viewer in the action. *Duel* gave him the opportunity to plunge the viewer into the fears, emotions and actions of the main character. He systematized this style in his subsequent film career. The specific tools he uses in pursuit of immersion, along with their most famous film appearance in his oeuvre, I list as follows: 1) subjective point of view shots extended in time (*Duel*); 2) shocking change of image scale (the shark emerges in *Jaws*); 3) overwhelming action left, right and center (crowd scenes in *Jaws*); 4) dimensional sound effects (*Raiders of the Lost Ark*); 5) bathing the audience in light (God's light in *Close Encounters of the Third Kind*); 6) and much later he used a chaotic hand-held camera (*Schindler's List*), 7) computer enhancement (*Jurassic Park*) and 8) desaturated color (*Saving Private Ryan*) to overwhelm the spectators. While the last two would need advances in technology not available in the 1970s, a thorough analysis would establish that the first six tools had already been deployed in Spielberg's early television work. Examples would include the off-screen typewriting sound in *Colombo* as an early use of dimensional sound. The flare from the sun in various shots in *Duel* anticipates the blinding lights of *Close Encounters*. There i⸱⸱⸱ camera movement leading David Ma⸱ the bathroom in *Duel* that prefigures held shots of the Omaha Beach scenes i point is that Spielberg recycles shots and his career (as do all film directors), but taught him to be most interested in what he could do to pull the viewer into the experience of even a small image. It is a philosophy of visual storytelling; at various times this philosophy will determine his choice of which stories to tell.

Perhaps *The Sugarland Express* was a poor choice for his first film. The characters were too different from the audience to allow vicarious participation in the chase, even when Spielberg's camera invited them to do so. The story of young outlaw lovers versus state troopers reflected divisions in American society. Meanwhile the audience was reaching a point, after the civil rights campaign, Vietnam, and Watergate, where they seemed to reject such reflections. Instead Spielberg now committed to the idea that the heroes of his movies should be middling everymen: surrogates for the audience. The next batch of films was designed to invite participation: viewers could join the characters fighting sharks, encountering aliens, and having archaeological adventures. These films—from *Jaws* and *Raiders* to *Close Encounters* and *E.T.*—ostentatiously ignored the sociopolitical dimensions of life in favor of old Hollywood entertainment values mixed with a new hipness of camera and style. This papering over of divisions was of course a kind of politics, even though it was marketed as a respite from politics. The resulting popularity of his films put Spielberg right at the heart of the film industry, which was shedding both the discredited establishment and the brooding characters of New Hollywood.

In later years the producers Zanuck and Brown expressed disappointment with the returns of *The Sugarland Express*, but it was not a failed film. Its $2 million budget was slightly below the Motion Picture Association of America (MPAA) average and its global box office of almost $13 million earned a profit. It was merely in later years the producers learned the vastly superior potential returns of Spielberg's emerging formula. In any case they were distracted from *The Sugarland Express* by the overwhelming success of their other production that year: *The Sting*. Indeed, it may have been while Zanuck and Brown were counting their sting money that Spielberg swiped a novel off their desk. It was a yet-to-be-published manuscript called *Jaws*.

3

THE SHARK AND
THE BLOCKBUSTER

The successes of *The Godfather* and *American Graffiti* revealed audience interest in refreshed old genres. Spielberg had lived through the lessons of *Duel* (a success) and *The Sugarland Express* (a disappointment). It was natural for him to conclude that his talents were related to his ability to excite the audience with a "you are there" perspective, instead of building stories with hard-to-understand characters. It is Warren Buckland's insight that Spielberg innovated away from his immediate predecessors such as Penn or Nichols, and now threw his hat in with Coppola and Lucas. "The timing of [Spielberg's] entry into the New Hollywood was too late, as all the innovators had already made their contribution and sealed their reputations. . . . When he 'borrowed' the Jaws manuscript from Richard Zanuck's desk, he seized the opportunity to enter the film industry from a new tradition (the contemporary blockbuster) and as an innovator of that tradition" (Buckland, 84).

JAWS SWIMS AWAY FROM THE DISASTER CYCLE

Spielberg forged his innovation by trying to emulate Hitch-cock while competing with his contemporaries. The story of *Jaws* was simple in the extreme. It was about a white shark attacking swimmers at a Long Island beach resort. While it might attract a fan of Hitchcock thrillers such as *The Birds* (1963), the more proximate examples inspiring a major studio to produce the novel were disaster films such as *Airport* (1970), *The Poseidon Adventure* (1972) and *The Towering Inferno* (1974). Stephen Keane distinguishes this cycle from previous movies set amidst catastrophe. "[the 1970s cycle] tend to take place in contemporary settings [mostly in California] and the characters represent a cross section of American society. Class conflict is a major resulting factor in this respect and further representative clashes are engendered by the isolated settings and situations" (13).

The disaster cycle covers many movies with a variety of structures but the top end, represented by *Airport*, *The Poseidon Adventure*, and *The Towering Inferno*, all featured ensemble casts. The advertising for each film would display a banner that had thumbnail portraits of eight to ten actors. The one-sheet poster for *Airport* has a dozen such portraits, as do images in advertising for *The Towering Inferno* and *The Poseidon Adventure*. Amazingly, practically all the dozen or so stars would be prominent enough to be known to a sizable percentage of the audience. Half the pleasure of watching the films was anticipating which star would be cast against type and who would die in the film. These movies made a lot of money and may have in themselves represented the emergence of a new level of profit-making in the American film industry. But they were not part of New Hollywood. Their look had more in common with the fading road show

The multiple images and thumbnail portraits of the stars in The Poseidon Adventure *are in contrast to the classic image in the* Jaws (see next page)

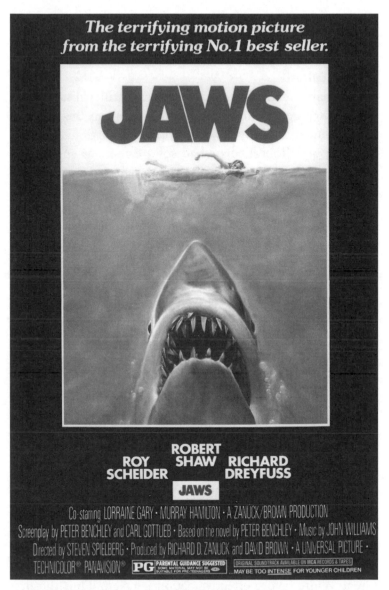

publicity of the single phallic shark about to devour the naked swimmer and the entire global movie industry. Photofest

formulas, such as marketing a large ensemble of stars. The stars had high profiles because many had been around for more than a decade. They were relics of a fading era in popular culture.

Spielberg had the instinct to make his thriller/disaster film for his own generation. He took it away from the imperial establishment of Hollywood by avoiding a cast of stars. Roy Scheider and Robert Shaw had solid careers as supporting actors. Richard Dreyfuss had emerged in *American Graffiti* but was not very prominent. They were the three leads who embody the old-fashioned class conflict built into Peter Benchley's novel *Jaws*. In addition, Spielberg urged his screenwriters to get away from the clichés of the disaster genre. They stripped the young scientist Matt Hooper (Dreyfuss) of the sexuality his character had in the novel. The character of the crusty old shark hunter Quint (Robert Shaw) was built up in the movie only to show that his actions were not effective despite his working-class experience. Instead, the surprising hero turned out to be the everyman: well-meaning middle-aged Sheriff Brody (Roy Scheider).[4]

The movie starts with a series of missteps by Brody, who yields to outrageous pressure from the town's mayor (Murray Hamilton) to keep the tourist beach open, even after evidence of a shark attack. The public officials are ineffective, even when the shark confirms its presence by killing again. The town takes little consideration of the greater public good when it meets to try to preserve as much of its summer beach business as possible. A bounty is offered that inspires a chaotic fish hunt by bumbling idiots. So much for collective action. The wrong shark is caught and another man is eaten by the Great White before effective action is taken. Thus the first half of the movie disposes of public action and public authority. In the second half, Quint takes Hooper and Brody out to sea on his fishing boat to find the marauding beast. They find the marauder, only to realize that they are not prepared for its size and ferocity. The shark eats Quint and sinks the boat just as Brody shoots a pressurized tank that blows the predator to pieces. A lost-at-sea Hooper reemerges and the two survivors swim back to land.

The movie's jaundiced view of local government mirrored a general loss of respect for authority. In only the previous year published transcripts revealed the meanness and law-breaking environment of the presidency. Nixon had resigned from office in disgrace in August 1974 and now government officials were fair game even for mainstream entertainment. But it was somewhat surprising that *Jaws* represented out-of-shape middle-aged fishermen as ineffective stumblers. Were the filmmakers playing a generational game, by flattering the younger members of the audience? Spielberg went to some effort to cast a young Dreyfuss as the smart biological scientist. Yet that flattery stopped in the second half. Despite Hooper's smarts, he could not handle the shark.

The hero was not Quint, the working-class relic, either. He was crude, sexist, and a strict enforcer of a hierarchy of labor. Neither Hooper nor, by extension, the film's director would forgive him his patriarchal ways. He had survived a shark attack in World War Two after the sinking of the U.S.S. Indianapolis. Now, more than forty years later, his obsession was approaching the level of Captain Ahab, the doomed protagonist of Herman Melville's nineteenth-century novel *Moby Dick*. Coincidentally, this novel was again in vogue in the 1970s. *Moby Dick* had become "the one literary allusion that most often surfaces in the Vietnam War literature and film" (Palmer, 78). *Jaws* was not part of this Vietnam War literature but it was unconsciously borrowing the tropes of this time of transition. The film's characterization of Quint touched upon the passing of the labor movement and the working class that fought World War Two.

Old labor's refusal to support anti-war advocates was a fatal weakening of the progressive movement. Younger workers became disillusioned with their union leaders. From this perspective Quint became the receptacle for the counterculture's dislike of the old labor movement.

The shark's first victim was the primal erotic taboo: the naked girl. The last killing was when the fish almost gleefully devours the old salty seaman. Almost simultaneously, Sheriff Brody, the family man, kills the shark. It would be odd for a New Hollywood film to pick a policeman for the hero. Was Spielberg throwing his hat in with the older members of the audience that go to the disaster movies? But Brody is no strutting law-and-order hero; he is a barely competent average person. Sheriff Brody was an extension of David Mann from *Duel*. The actors, Roy Scheider and Dennis Weaver, were similar in their demeanor and their uncertain body movement. Spielberg shot them in analogous style. While the camera pivoted around David Mann traveling in his car, it dollied in to Brody's reaction to his environment. Using deep focus, Spielberg placed Brody in the foreground, watching for the shark, while in the background everyone else frolicked without regard to the danger.

The sheriff was isolated in his reactions and therefore was just as unsure of himself as Mann. The extreme foreground/background shot was repeated several times in the first half of the movie, setting up its payoff during the hunt, when Brody was tossing chum into the sea. He was crammed into an uncomfortable close-up on the right-hand side of the screen, a close-up that seems unjustified by the action until the shark emerges out of the sea on the left-hand side, shocking audiences in the first great reveal of the all-too-solid monster that has terrorized them for an hour and twenty minutes.

Sheriff Brody is about to see something.

The relationship of Brody, Quint, and Hooper is not the reason for the runaway success of *Jaws*. But the representation of the relationship is a visible indicator of the director's desire to stitch together his own generation and everyone else as members of an all-inclusive audience. Because of this the film feels fresh in comparison to the ensemble-driven relations in the previous disaster films.

The immersive style comes to fruition in *Jaws*. First and foremost is the authenticity of the experience. Spielberg insisted that he had to shoot in the waters of the Northeast coast. Just as in *Duel*, Spielberg fought with the producers and the old Hollywood special-effects people to take his camera out on location. The producers wanted to work in a large sea tank. But Spielberg stood his ground in order to make sure he could get the viewers to participate in the action. It cost a lot of time and money but increasingly he had the self-confidence to refuse to be satisfied with old movie tricks that he judged as too cheesy.

Once he won that fight, the rest was of a piece. He was able to delay production in order to get a decent mechanical shark and again refused to compromise. Both of these battles were fights to upgrade the status of the genre. Universal may have thought that this was just a "B" movie thriller without the expense of an all-star disaster-movie cast, but Spielberg convinced his producers to spend the savings on special effects since the movie was going to be a big winner. They let him move his camera and use complicated changes of visual scale in order to tell his story and shock the audience. Spielberg also got to work with the music composer John Williams, and they have worked consistently together on every Spielberg movie since. In all matters the young twenty-something director won the fight to treat a thriller as if it was going to be the biggest movie of the year.

It became the biggest movie in ten years.

Jaws *was a true blockbuster with lines around the block. A photo from the original 1975 release in NYC.*

A New Era

Star Wars surpassed it two years later. *Jaws* and *Star Wars* are the start of the blockbuster era in Hollywood. The astronomical grosses that these movies made marked the beginning of a new period. As shown in Table 3.1, *Jaws* inaugurated an era where the top films earned twice as much as the top films had previously. While *Jaws* holds up well after thirty years of viewing, its historic status as the movie that marked a turning point remains a surprise. Why did it become a phenomenon? Why did it break all box office records in motion picture history, and why does it still remain in the top 40 movie earners of all time? The movie did not announce itself as the great American epic, as did *Gone With the Wind* (1939); the production delays did not capture a fraction of the media attention that *Titanic* (1996) did. The movie was self-assuredly well made and the studio was gung-ho, but no more so than with dozens of others. Its earnings were soon superseded by *Star Wars* (a movie that was more epic in scope and yet less well crafted) and several others over the next few years. This suggests that *Jaws* crystallized gathering forces in the film industry more than it created new forces. It finally brought together an audience that wanted to go to the movie theaters and had already done so in larger and larger numbers for *The Godfather* and *The Exorcist* (1973). Those movies also increased the budgets for supposedly lowly genres. *Jaws* and subsequently *Star Wars* got everyone to go once, and preteen and teenage boys to go time after time. The repeat viewers became the audience that built the blockbuster.

North American filmgoers paid $260 million to see *Jaws*; Universal Studios collected $130 million from their ticket sales. This was 58 percent higher than any previous film in the decade. *Jaws* accounted for 12.3 percent of the North American box office in that year. One would have to go back

Table 3.1 EARNINGS OF NUMBER ONE US MOVIES 1963–1985[1]

Year	Title	North American rentals[2] ($ millions) for the top movie	North American box office ($ millions) for the top movie	North American box office total ($ millions) for all movies
1963	Cleopatra	26	52	942
1964	My Fair Lady	34	68	951
1965	Sound of Music	80	160	1,067
1966	Doctor Zhivago	47	112	1,119
1967	The Graduate	44	105	1,128
1968	Love Bug	23	51[3]	1,294
1969	Butch Cassidy	46	102	1,400
1970	Airport	45	100	1,429
1971	Love Story	49	106	1,350
1972	The Godfather	87	135	1,583
1973	Exorcist	89	165	1,524
1974	The Towering Inferno	49	116	1,909
1975	Jaws	130	260	2,115
1976	Rocky	57	117	2,036
1977	Star Wars	194	323	2,372
1978	Grease	96	210	2,643
1979	Kramer vs. Kramer	60	106	2,821
1980	Empire Strikes Back	142	223	2,749
1981	Raiders	116	242	2,960
1982	ET	229	400	3,445
1983	Return of the Jedi	169	263	3,766
1984	Beverly Hills Cop	108	238	4,031
1985	Back to the Future	105	208	3,749

[1] Rental and box office figures come from various issues of *Variety*. The box office total comes from annual issues of *Economic Review of the Motion Picture Association of America*. While all figures are unreliable there is agreement within the industry that these figures do accurately measure the relative earnings of movies vis à vis each other.
[2] Rentals are the percentage of the box office that the distributing movie studio actually earns. The box office is the total amount of money spent on admissions. The difference between the two figures is what the theater itself receives in revenues.
[3] www.starpulse.com/movies downloaded October 3, 2007.

to *The Sound of Music* in 1965 to find a film that dominated its year to the same degree (15 percent).

Some of these unprecedented figures are explained by ticket prices steadily rising 35 percent from $2.05 in 1975 to $2.78 in 1981. The era of the blockbuster movie was the era where the top movies captured a greater share of the total box office than before *Jaws*. The total revenue for studios climbed also, at a gradual although steady and satisfying rate. Total admissions for all movies fluctuated, plus or minus 5 percent, around one billion dollars in those same years. It was the top films that really jump-started earnings up into the stratosphere. This inspired the studios to invest more money in producing and marketing the potential big-money films. The pattern of hits showed the studios that the likeliest winning genre was action/adventure, attracting vicarious thrill-seekers. Thus began the critique that films increasingly eroded narrative sophistication in favor of building up pleasures of the spectacle, such as car chases and acts of explosive destruction.

Ironically, an extremely effective marketing strategy was designed for *Jaws* precisely because the movie was not prestigious. Nobody suggested a road show roll-out. The producers were not going to treat this the way they treated their previous star-studded hit *The Sting*, with a high-stakes Christmas release in New York and Los Angeles. Zanuck and Brown had bought a summer thriller novel. *Jaws* was designed to be released as widely as possible and to make its money quickly. Indeed, because of its subject matter, it was to be released in the summer, a season that was traditionally shunned by big movies as a time when there were too many other leisure activities for movies to compete effectively. The only new competition *Jaws* had in the theater on June 20, 1975, was the dead-on-arrival *Once is Not Enough* (1975), based on a novel by Jacqueline Susanne.

TV MARKETING

Universal believed *Jaws* would be a quick winner and invested accordingly in a high-stakes television advertising campaign. It had learned a lesson from Tom Laughlin's use of TV in his 1973 release of *Billy Jack*. Lew Wasserman, the legendary CEO of MCA/Universal, consulted with Laughlin several times about the innovative releases of the Billy Jack series (Hayes and Bing, 280). Hollywood was just now embracing TV advertising after shunning it for most of the 1950s and 1960s. Although the medium was a natural for movies, as it could show stunning visuals, the logistics for TV advertising were not considered favorable. It was expensive and it was hard to correlate national TV campaigns with specific neighborhood theater showings. It was also assumed that the audiences were different. Columbia Pictures was the first studio to try television marketing. Universal decided to take the plunge into TV advertising by tying it to a wide release of the movie. The initial plan was for 600 theaters but Wasserman actually cut back on the number of initial theaters to less than 500, still a relatively high number. The marketing department spent $700,000 on network TV advertisements, Their overall campaign of $2.5 million was 67 percent larger than the MPAA average (Hayes and Bing, 158).

The movie had an impressive and significant image to sustain such an advertising campaign: a huge shark coming up from the bottom to swallow a tiny woman swimming blithely. Neither the movie nor the trailer revealed her frontal nudity but all the images in the TV and print marketing suggested enough to allow the audience to be tantalized by a promise of eroticized horror. The trailer and TV spots also managed to reproduce the sense of terror that Spielberg had given to the ocean by not showing the shark. The spot editors used threatening POV shots: the camera approached dangling legs of swimmers below the surface of the water. The suggestion of an impending shark attack was as effective in the TV advertisements enticing viewers as it was in the actual movie. It was a pioneering instance of the visceral moving image that played well on both the big and small screens. The TV advertising for *Star Wars* would use the same power of the moving camera when spots were built using the space jets' dogfights and attack on the Death Star.

In 1977 George Lucas completed his own parallel journey to Steven Spielberg. They had met in 1968 when Spielberg was showing *Amblin'* on the USC campus where Lucas was studying to be a filmmaker. Lucas's early efforts such as *THX 1138* (1971) showed some aspiration to art film experimentalism, yet his first fully financed movie, *American Graffiti*, was more nostalgic and less alienated than its European inspiration.[5] His next film was his own original story: *Star Wars*. There was no European inspiration for this one. The motivation was to fill a void that Hollywood had left in the previous decade when the studios turned away from fantasy and epic themes. Lucas simply used mythic archetypes. The result was a film that did not challenge anyone on an ideological level.

But the thrill level in *Star Wars* was taken to a degree that challenged even the old hands at Hollywood. He had first hired the special effects experts from *2001: A Space Odyssey*, but they faded away. A crew of less experienced men stuck to the difficult task of recreating the swoops and dives of space jets engaged in dogfights against images of stars and space. Lucas was hoping new computer technology would ease the task but the computers of the time could not deliver precisely what he wanted and so other techniques were improvised. They slowly put together fast-moving shots of spaceships and worked out visual techniques to get the audience on the edge of their seats. In the first shot Princess Leia's starship enters the shot from above and the audience adjusts to its size. The heart-pounding begins when the pursuing Imperial starship enters the same frame, and is revealed to be a couple of magnitudes larger as it takes up the entire screen. The change of scale may have been borrowed from some of the shocking shots of the shark in *Jaws*; it certainly becomes a cliché of the new wave of blockbusters. Surprisingly, it does not lose its power even by the time of *Independence Day* (1996), twenty years later. In 1977 the audience was enchanted and the film captured the hearts of an entire generation.

The two movies had changed the American movie industry. If *Jaws* had come after *Star Wars* it would have been a very profitable afterthought. There is no doubt that *Star Wars* was a thing in itself that would have changed the movie industry whatever the context into which it was launched. *Jaws'* event status depended more on luck: stumbling onto an empty summer; perfectly touching a national mood for a thriller that did not last long. This does not detract from its status as a social phenomenon. Its director was about to prove that he could put together phenomena again and again through the coming decades.

An Alien World: Close Encounters

Spielberg had not been resting on his laurels. He had used his white-hot status to push an idea he had had since childhood into a major big-budget movie. He signed a deal in 1973 with Columbia Pictures to develop a script for a film about unidentified flying objects (UFOs), aliens, and ordinary people. Spielberg's initial pitch linked UFOs and the political trauma of Watergate. McBride writes that an unusually high degree of collective distress in the American psyche over Vietnam and Watergate was causing a revival of interest in

UFOs (264). This is two years before the success of *Jaws* and Spielberg might surmise that the audience wanted overt resonance between politics and stories about outer space. But the path forward after *Jaws* was away from such a direct relationship between politics and entertainment. The director approached Paul Schrader, a writer and future director with a distinct dark vision, to write a draft. Schrader's draft dropped the political angle in favor of a religious journey. Spielberg was disappointed and dropped most of Schrader's ideas in favor of a story of an ordinary suburban man caught up in a quest to actually personally have an encounter with aliens.

The resulting film, *Close Encounters of the Third Kind*, still has political overtones. The UFO phenomenon has been constantly denied by the official United States government. The movie depicts aspects of this official denial. Spielberg softens the government's patriarchal and dismissive attitude towards UFO believers, however. Behind the scenes, military men and scientists unite with admirable openmindedness to investigate strange signals from outer space. There is some government manipulation of the investigation, particularly by the military. They refuse to let people participate or know about the strange signals. Instead, the government evacuates most of Wyoming by falsely claiming a nerve gas leak. But this manipulation is not sinister. It is softened by the lead French scientist, Claude Lacombe (François Truffaut), who allows the civilian Roy Neary (Richard Dreyfuss) and his companions inside the restricted perimeter. This story does not ask the audience to take a particularly negative view of the government but maintained Spielberg's man of authority as the man in the middle. Lacombe follows the pattern of Capt. Tanner and Sheriff Brody.

The film is harsh (as much as Spielberg can be harsh) in its treatment of suburbia. Neary is an Indiana utility repairman. He lives in a community that looks just as much like

Spielberg's sunbelt as it does the Midwest. He becomes a believer in UFOs after seeing them at close range. Neary constructs a sculpture in the day room of an image in his head of a mountain. This image turns out to be a precise image of Devil's Tower in Wyoming. The implication is that the aliens transmitted this image to him in order to inspire him to come to their rendezvous there. Despite Neary's behavior, he is never crazy and is quite capable of reason and sympathy towards his fellow UFOers and, in particular, Jillian Guiler (Melinda Dillon), whose son was abducted by the aliens. But his wife treats his nonconformist vision as a threat to the family and the children. She takes the children away and abandons him. This is a portrait of a man frustrated by the limited imagination of those around him, in both his family and his neighborhood.

Nonetheless, the social critique is a minor subtheme, as trivial as the "enemy of the people" fight between Brody and the Mayor in *Jaws*. The main point of the movie is the landing of the mothership bearing the aliens. This is the set that drove up the budget to just shy of $20 million and this is the payoff for all the effects that had the audience marvel at the scale of UFOs. Spielberg uses an array of immersive techniques such as the moving camera and extensive POV shots. This time he perfects what he called "God Lights." He had been unafraid to burn out portions of the shot with severe overlighting while maintaining proper exposure on a character or object since his early childhood films. This time he closely associated such lighting with the sublime, the awe of encountering something from another world. The power of the light bouncing off the movie screen baths the audience in its warmth. Like the visceral effect of the moving camera, it becomes a physical experience for the audience, more direct and more irresistible than mere photographic representation. It is fitting that as a child, he learned the power of such

"God Lights" refers to intense backlighting. This is a scene from Close Encounters. *Kobal*

lighting effects during a Jewish religious service (Morris, 8). While he had used it occasionally before, it becomes a motif in *Close Encounters* from the first time Neary senses the aliens to the final mothership scene where Spielberg uses it effectively to obscure the exact features of the aliens. From this point on in his career it will be part of his language, and he will use it on every film.

When *Close Encounters* was first proposed in 1973, the budget numbers were very small. Since *Jaws* showed what could happen with bigger budgets, Columbia agreed to more money as Spielberg's vision expanded. The studio did so even as it was teetering on the edge of bankruptcy. The demand for expensive and better effects was now part of the strategy to get the audience to participate in the magic of the film. Columbia executives doubled down and covered the growing budget. The showman Spielberg pulled it off and *Close Encounters of the Third Kind* grossed $166 million in North

America and another $172 million overseas, marking the first time a Spielberg movie made more money outside the United States than in it. (It should be noted that German financiers helped Columbia complete the film. Perhaps their interest led to more energetic distribution in Europe.) It was a remarkable achievement that helped save Columbia Pictures.

STRATEGIES OF THE CONTEMPORARY BLOCKBUSTER

Chris Jordan discusses the difference between the block-buster era and its predecessor, New Hollywood, as the revival of genre. He uses Robin Wood's analysis of the incoherent texts that implied a radical critique of society (*Texas Chainsaw Massacre*, 1974; *Taxi Driver*, 1980; and *Cruising*, 1980) as the receding wave of filmmaking. The incoming wave of "Lucas and Spielberg papered over the fissures and cracks created by the counter-culture" (55). It can be disputed whether *Jaws* had quite filled in all the fissures and cracks needed to launch the new wave.[6] Nonetheless, the combination of *Jaws/Star Wars/Close Encounters* establishes beyond dispute that the first cycle of the blockbusters was dominated by Spielberg/Lucas and that they were making stories for the whole audience that no longer focused on rebellion and alienation but on wonder and splendor.

Jaws and the others were a revival of Walt Disney's use of television to market his films. *The Wonderful World of Disney* in the 1950s was the first instance of cross-media marketing and media convergence. Disney had targeted young people who were still in their family homes watching television. But Disney never made a thriller with quite the shock factor of *Jaws*. The two 1977 films—*Close Encounters of the Third Kind* and *Star Wars*—made it clear that the blockbuster formula was to use Disney's cross-media marketing to get at a much wider audience. Some compared blockbuster stories to Disney but Krämer (2002) makes it clear that both Lucas and Spielberg wanted to differentiate themselves from Disney's 1950s emphasis on children's films in order to seek an all-age audience. He points out that Spielberg had dropped "When You Wish Upon a Star" from the ending of *Close Encounters* because of the song's overly close association with Disney.

Old Hollywood used genre to target niche audiences. One primary example was Disney using fairy tales to target children. The new directors were combining the various niche audiences into larger combined crowds by reinvigorating action and other genres. They were doing this by insisting on real locations, state-of-the-art special effects, fast-paced editing techniques, and immersive camera style. They were blending genres. The writers for *Jaws* had married an adult theme ("enemy of the people") with the terror of a shark attack. Lucas had imparted a space adventure with mythic structure and some New Age philosophy of holistic forces versus dark impulses. *Close Encounters* spared nothing to give adults as well as children the awe of a visit from outer space. This trend continued and deepened. These filmmakers were cognizant of the generational divide in cultural attitudes and therefore used genre blending to mitigate the polarizing political landscape of the times. Meanwhile those who continued to use marginal genres such as horror and crime to eke out an income from smaller theaters saw their audiences pulled away. Now they had to compete with major studios coming in and appropriating these types of stories by increasing the budgets and the sophistication of the scripts (McCarthy, 22).

For example, until 1978 Superman was strictly a comic-book hero for boys. In that year Alexander Salkind produced the movie *Superman* as a contemporary blockbuster (it was the second top earner for the year). He did so by hiring the writers for *Bonnie and Clyde* to do the script. David Newman and Robert Benton worked hard to sexualize Superman and to otherwise intrigue adult viewers as well as younger ones.[7] The marketing emphasized the realism of the special effects by using the tagline "You'll believe a man can fly." Newman remembers that this tagline was designed to attract the adult moviegoer.[8] Salkind also went to great, indeed humiliating, effort to cast Marlon Brando for the same reason: to expand the appeal of the story beyond the traditional audience for comic-book heroes.

In one way or another, the new movies were hybrid genres that were pushing the American film industry to unprecedented revenue levels. By the time *Close Encounters* was released in November of 1977, *Star Wars* had surpassed *Jaws'* box office records. It was remarkable that the Spielberg science fiction film could make so much money while Lucas's film was still in the theaters. The audience seemed insatiable. *Star Wars* took 22 percent of its year's box office (while *Close Encounters* got another 7 percent). The *Jaws/Star Wars/Close Encounters* trend was confirmed when *Grease* reached this same stratosphere in 1978. 1979 was a brief return to normal earnings, but *The Empire Strikes Back* received 1980 rentals in excess of $209 million and *Raiders of the Lost Ark* did the same in 1981. Both films captured over 8 percent of the total domestic box office. Their earning power defined these blockbusters.

Studios were newly willing to spend more money on production and marketing for the anticipated top films. Mass media became obsessed with box office numbers. Starting with *Jaws*, print outlets such as *Time* and *Newsweek* breathlessly reported how the films were breaking box office records. This new attention was helped by changes in the computerization of news gathering. The quick and accurate reporting fed the growing trend in mainstream newspapers to report box office figures as a news item (Wasser, 2001, 168). Their readers became naturally curious about such a popular-culture phenomenon and went out to see what all the fuss was about—by attending the movies. In this way movies became events. Movies had been events before but usually for reasons more closely tied to their content than their earnings. There was the ambitious scope (and racist ideology) of *Birth of a Nation* (1915). *Gone With The Wind* (1939) built upon its source, a best-selling epic romance, to get an entire nation interested in its glamorous stars even before the cameras started to roll. 1956's *The Ten Commandments* tied in with the recent creation of Israel. In contrast, the regularity of event films starting with *Jaws* gave these phenomena more the characteristics of pseudo-events—only famous because they are famous. People were interested in these movies only because other people were interested.

If people who bought tickets were interested in the earnings, the people who actually pocketed the earnings were even more interested. The industry's rhetoric turned towards the big earners. The director Gary Ross remembers being around his father's filmmaking buddies in the 1950s and observing that that they "did not talk about the box office gross of their films; it was considered coarse" (Hayes and Bing, 366). Of course old Hollywood cared about money, but it was easier to be discreet about financial matters when earnings were more evenly distributed among the various films. Now the great disparities generated much discussion and feelings of competition and envy.

INFLUENCE OF FILM

The status of film was changing again. Previously, film had yielded its position as the primary medium of American entertainment to television in the 1950s as box office declined while broadcasting ratings increased. The decline continued slowly as Hollywood lost its relevancy to teenaged audiences; then the moviegoing public was splintered when New Hollywood reclaimed relevancy by embracing the anti-hero. In 1974, the year before *Jaws*, the leading magazine company, Time-Life, launched its new and soon to be most successful magazine. They called it *People*. It was a combination of human-interest and celebrity stories. Richard Stolley was the first managing editor. He issued the following hierarchical formula for this mainstream journal of American popular culture: "young was better than old, pretty was better than ugly, television was better than music, music was better than movies, movies was better than sports and anything was better than politics" (Benzel, 36).

Movies were only number three? Television was first? Music was second? This is a surprising ranking from today's perspective. Stolley had an intriguing and credible list of what Americans were paying attention to in the early 1970s on the cusp of the blockbuster era. American TV had awakened from its irrelevancy in 1971 with an earthshaker: *All in the Family* was based on *Til Death Us Do Part* (BBC, 1965–1975) and like the British version, it featured loud arguments between a bigoted father and a progressive son-in-law over the political and social issues of the times. It became the number one show in America for a time. Norman Lear produced *All in the Family* and went on to create a series of sitcoms, including some of the first to feature African Americans on prime time: *Sanford and Son*, *The Jeffersons* and *Good Times*. At the same time the relatively bland *The Mary Tyler Moore Show* (CBS 1970–1977) was a breakthrough for its portrayal of a single professional woman.

Sports were becoming a small-screen spectacle. In September 1970 Roone Arledge brought football to prime time with *Monday Night Football* (ABC 1970–2005). This show steadily increased the emphasis on colorful commentary and graphics, giving the sport more of the trappings of entertainment. Considering this development plus the interest in TV news, it is not so surprising for a magazine editor to rank the small screen first. The second ranking went to music, which had lost some of its counterculture clout with the waning of the great turmoil of the sixties. The top musicians were still making money, however, from both their appearances and their record sales. Rock was so popular and so well marketed that many questioned individual rock stars' pretensions to authenticity and to participating in the same lifestyle as their listeners. By the late 1970s the overproduction of rock inspired a punk reaction: newcomers claimed only simple skills as musicians and performers in order to convey passion and glorify marginality. In a similar rise and fall, fictional television lost some of its newfound relevancy as Norman Lear gave way to Fred Silverman as the guiding light of prime time, later in the decade. Silverman promiscuously promoted anything that would grab attention. He was responsible both for the scantily clad eye candy of *Charlie's Angels* (ABC 1976–1980) and the first extended prime-time presentation of African American history in *Roots* (ABC 1977). In 1976 he also changed the direction of *Happy Days* (ABC 1974–1984) and made it a ratings success. *Happy Days* started as the TV version of *American Graffiti*. In the cultural hierarchy TV was once again following the movies.

Stolley made his statement that movies were in third place before Spielberg and Lucas had placed movies back at the center of American popular culture. The mid-1970s movies fit right in with a general cultural movement towards spectacle over narrative. Big rock stage shows and power chords drowned out the message of the lyrics (if there were any). *Charlie's Angels'* nubile bodies made a mockery of the TV crime genre. Sports were now staged for the cameras. More and more graphic displays were being used to provide visual excitement for TV news. By the early 1980s Caldwell has detected a general shift towards visual pleasures in TV; he has coined the term "televisuality" to describe the period. Thus the coincidence of spectacle in several media reveals a homology of the times. Lucas's quote in the opening of the previous chapter suggests that all media were now looking to visual gimmicks to crank the adrenaline for a new generation. It was an easier mission to accomplish in the movies than on TV or even at the rock concert. The young film directors were about to take the adrenaline even further in a collaborative effort between the two wunderkinds.

These cultural transformations showed that the 1960s youth movement had metamorphosed into 1970s mobile privatization. In 1974 Raymond Williams described trends in technology that "served at once mobile and home-centered" ways of living (20). His words were remarkably prescient, considering the subsequent adoption of home video, laserdisc, boom boxes, cassette and CD music, personal computers and the internet. These technologies were steps toward the creation of a transnational media system.

The new markets subtly influenced the film directors. At first even film producers and financiers did not understand the profound changes that were coming. Sidney Sheinberg actually initiated an ultimately unsuccessful copyright infringement case on behalf of Universal against Sony for its VCR. He could not see that within a dozen years the VCR would return more money to Hollywood than the movie theaters. Other executives were not that aggressively hostile, although they ignored the VCR while hoping that cable channels such as HBO would make them richer. Steven Spielberg himself loved gadgets but was too much of a lover of big-screen movies to be very happy about more people watching his movies on the small screen. Nonetheless, when the time came, his movies would be as big videocassette sellers as they were box office attractions. The technological expansion of movie distribution was well underway and this, rather than increased attendance, would radically expand the revenues of the movie industry, both here and overseas.

In the 1960s movie theaters on both sides of the Atlantic had been allowed to deteriorate. The blockbusters inspired a round of rebuilding on both sides of the ocean. The blockbuster also coincided with the division of movie theaters into many different mini-theaters with smaller screens. The initial impulse to "multiplex" the theaters was to give consumers more choices. But the logic of blockbuster distribution was not more choices of titles, since only the big-budget films got the attention. Soon the choice multiplexes offered consumers was convenience; more start times for the blockbuster of the week, not a greater diversity of films.

The age of the blockbuster neatly coincides with the decline of a mass American audience for foreign films. The foreign films still had 7.3 percent of the US box office in the year of *Jaws*. They only had 3 percent in the year of *Star Wars*. If we look at five-year averages, we see the average import share of US box office for 1971–1975 was almost 7 percent. It dropped by more than a third to 4.4 percent in 1976–1980. It stayed at that level for 1981–1985 and then dropped by 40 percent to 2.5 percent and lower for the 1990s (Foreign Flix).

RAIDERS AND CLASSIC HOLLYWOOD

Just as *Star Wars* was earning its big money and *Close Encounters* was entering post-production, Lucas and Spielberg met on a Hawaiian vacation. They concocted the idea of working together on an action/adventure film. Their common language was film itself. Spielberg expressed his regret over not being able to direct a James Bond movie while Lucas talked of his hopes to revive the Saturday matinee genre of serial adventures, to which he used to love to go. They decided to formulate a movie based on a Bond-like figure undertaking boyish matinee-type adventures. They agreed to use their power to demand a better position for sharing the profits. Lucas wanted a contract where the studio would actually be partners with the filmmakers and would share all revenues, even the distribution fee, and they started shopping their proposal around the various studios. Despite their proven earning power, the studios were reluctant. While this deal was still brewing Spielberg went out and directed *1941* (1979).

The film starts with a Japanese submarine cruising off Los Angeles shortly after Pearl Harbor. Meanwhile the onshore Californians try to mobilize and organize their defenses. Things spin quickly out of control as young soldiers chase young women and the adults display their utter incompetency. The Japanese also have a hard time. They cannot find a suitable target. An army tank plunges into a paint store. Night falls. A riot breaks out at the USO dance. Wild Bill Kelso (John Belushi) flies his fighter plane down Santa Monica Boulevard, causing mayhem. The submarine fires one torpedo and leaves. Morning dawns. Ward Douglas (Ned Beatty) celebrates the survival of his house by pounding a wreath onto the door. The house then falls into the sea. End credits roll.

1941 was a satire written by two younger protégés of Spielberg. It was a stretch for the young director who had never handled comedy or satire before on television or film. He had also not handled a historical setting before, but that is rarely a strong consideration in a satire. Successful satire is motivated by anger at the present. Robert Zemeckis hinted that his writerly vision was darker, more cynical than the resulting film.[9]

But the movie was not an angry movie. Spielberg and his writers never thought to find fault with the characters' infantile reactions. They did not want to make sour observations about the national character. They only wanted to indulge the audience's desire for mayhem. Everything was played for laughs. There was no acknowledgment of the racism that led to the zoot suit riots or the unconstitutional internment of Japanese-Americans. Sexism was presented as sexy. The film had massive scenes of harmless destruction, and other borrowings from the previous year's hit directed by John Landis, which was a frat-boy riot called *Animal House*. But with ten times the budget it only did half the business. *1941* was a financial and critical disappointment (North American box office gross of $32 million). This time Spielberg's instinct for audience flattery failed to attract. The film did better overseas and writers and director agree in their DVD commentaries twenty years later that the foreigners probably gave a darker interpretation to the movie.

There was about a two-year gap between *1941* and *Raiders*. Lucas agreed to produce and Spielberg to direct *Raiders of the Lost Ark* when they finalized their profit-sharing deal with Paramount Pictures. The director was very agreeable to restraints and tips that Lucas insisted on as producer, because Spielberg wanted to renew his commitment to craft, just as he had done previously when he was too experimental in making episodic television. Both men wanted to make an old-fashioned film, once again showing their instinct for the American audience. The culture had shifted right in these two years and the tried-and-true was once again a virtue. After all, the new president was now a seventy-year-old Republican.

The long American Thermidorean reaction to a welfare state and expansion of individual rights reached a landmark with the November 1980 election of Ronald Reagan to the presidency. The United States had never gone as far as comparable advanced countries in expanding government responsibilities for welfare and regulation and now the Reagan administration was going to slowly roll back even the few government programs and regulations that were in place. The political leadership encouraged Americans to look inward, to lead more private lives, to demand little from the government or other public institutions. The tone of the administration was interesting in light of Ronald Reagan's past connection with show business. Reagan was a former actor (and a former client of Lew Wasserman, Spielberg's mentor and boss at Universal). Reagan presented the Republican agenda in a genial fashion. He had a way of delivering absolutely nasty lines such as "The nine most terrifying words in the English language are, 'I'm from the government and I'm here to help'" with a broad Hollywood smile that robbed the line of its confrontational bite. Even liberal Democrats in the media industries felt little animosity and had no need to fight the administration. Reagan, for better or worse, influenced American popular culture to embrace his rosy view of American triumphalism.

For example, a tolerant liberal such as Spielberg did not view the Reagan revolution as a direct challenge to his beliefs. Reagan even invited Spielberg to show *Close Encounters* at the White House. The director dutifully showed up with his film and managed to conceal his astonishment when a personal comment by Reagan implied that the President also believed the government was covering up UFOs (McBride, 266). Even if Spielberg was a lifelong Democrat, who had opposed the Vietnam War and supported ethnic diversity, there was a streak of sunbelt provincialism in the filmmaker that was cut from the same cloth as President Reagan. It came out strongly in the first two Indiana Jones movies.

The first in the series is *Raiders of the Lost Ark*. Indiana Jones is a slightly disreputable professor of archaeology who engaged in many adventures in his fieldwork. He is approached by the American government in the years before World War Two to covertly frustrate the German Nazi project to recover the lost ark of the Jewish covenant, which may have mystical powers. Jones recruits a former (and still bitter) girlfriend, Marion Ravenswood (Karen Allen), to help find the ark and immediately crosses the path of the Nazis who alternately beat him up, capture her, capture him, and allow both to escape. In between fighting, escaping and being captured, Jones teams up with an old friend, Sallah (John Rhys-Davis), in Cairo and fights off hordes of Arabic kidnappers (allied with the Germans). They find the ark but cannot hold on to it after the Nazis discover their whereabouts. Jones and Ravenswood then have to slip aboard the German submarine that is carrying the prize. They reclaim it for the good guys after the Germans thoughtlessly open it up and are destroyed by the mystical powers within the ark. The final shot is of the US government storing the mystical ark without fanfare in some endless warehouse.

The summer 1981 release of *Raiders of the Lost Ark* confirmed Lucas and Spielberg's close relationship with the American audience. The film grossed $242 million in the domestic market, which works out to about 87 million tickets sold and makes it the third most popular Spielberg film to this date. It cemented the reputation of Spielberg as a skilled entertainer. The design of the movie was episodic, along the lines of the early matinees, but the entertainment values were much higher. The various action bits were not only spectacular and far above the ambitions of the matinees, there were many more of them, starting with the boulder about to crush Indiana Jones (Harrison Ford) and ending a hundred and ten minutes later with the spirits of the Lost Ark melting the Nazis. Spielberg's shot plan showed an extreme confidence in the classic language of Hollywood. It was full of foreshadowing and meaningful repetitions that alternately allowed the audience to decipher what has happened only after it has happened or told the audience what to expect before the protagonists find out.[10]

The film's relation with old Hollywood was not simply one of imitation. When Lucas and Spielberg had rescreened their childhood favorites, they realized that the actual films were tacky, not presentable to contemporary children or even their parents. They ended up filming in a new style to fulfill their childhood memories of excitement rather than duplicating the actual style of the movies that they had remembered. It was not just their memories but the memories of the older segment of the "all-age" audience. Therefore their quotes of earlier movies triggered the "telegraphic shorthand" that flattered audience knowledge of cinema as the accelerated pace took advantage of the increased familiarity the audience had with cinema's visual language. The Raiders' style relied heavily on the audiences' pre-existing view of the world as constructed by Hollywood.

Even though Lucas/Spielberg upgraded the production values of the old series, they neglected to upgrade the casual colonial attitudes that were embedded in the old Hollywood films. It was a surprising oversight, particularly since many films of the 1960s and 1970s had shown increasing sensitivity. The "white man's burden" image of Jones fighting off the Arabs was the most problematic act of thoughtlessness towards others. Spielberg kept up the killing action without explaining where these bad guys were coming from or why they were attacking. It became an extreme instance of what is called "happy violence": excessive representations of killing where there are no consequences to the hero. Spielberg put a mean blockbuster twist on it. An Arabic swordsman (Terry Richards) steps up to challenge Indiana Jones by twirling his scimitar. Jones responds with a grimace of exasperation, and then shoots the swordsman dead with his pistol. The swordsman never had a chance. Since the expected cliché learned from a lifetime of film watching is that the hero will somehow engage the swordsman in a fair confrontation, the casual unsportsmanlike shooting was a surprise to the audience, who generally were shocked into cheering and laughing at this scene. Previously, movie heroism consisted of winning against overwhelming odds. The fact that Spielberg used this bit (Harrison Ford had improvised it on the set) suggested that the filmmaker had absorbed some of the new win-by-any-means definition of heroism. This new mean-spirited hero became prominent in the cycle of action movies made by other directors in the wake of *Raiders*.

This film, more than the previous ones, melded the blockbuster into the Reagan ideology of resurgent America. A larger metaphor behind the action in *Raiders* was the American emotional desire to never lose again. This emotion prevailed among those who had opposed American participation in the Vietnam War as well as those who had supported it. When movies such as *Raiders* displayed this emotion, they enabled a lack of responsibility in the mainstream culture. After Vietnam, Americans still wanted to project power without risking American lives. The military did this in a series of overwhelming bombing actions against various enemies. Over the decade the bombing separated Americans from feeling any responsibility for the actions of the government and accepting as inevitable the loss of foreign civilian lives in overseas adventures. Naturally such an irresponsible people wanted their cultural artifacts to avoid the reality of history and instead treat the past as romantic fantasy. Indiana Jones shooting the

A Hollywood hero doesn't fight fair.

swordsman mirrored this perfectly, without forethought or consciousness.

Only after *1941* and *Raiders* would Spielberg develop a genuine interest in the historical film. History was not on the mind of moviemakers or moviegoers as the decade wore down. Not more than a handful of films set in the past had made it into the ranks of the top ten film earners since 1973. The historical impulse had faded with the end of the road show era, although the past setting had lingered due to a desire of the movie audience for nostalgia, as in *Summer of '42* (1971), *Lady Sings The Blues* (1972), and *The Sting* (1973). War films had lost their appeal. *Tora, Tora, Tora* (1970) was a disappointment while *Midway* (1976) was only a modest success. A trickle of Vietnam War films was just starting with *The Deer Hunter* (1978). It avoided provoking its audience by carefully restricting its story to the after-effects of war. It earned twice as much as *Coming Home*, a more politically committed Vietnam story released in the same year. All agreed that the industry was generally sour on politics and history, as *Raiders* climbed the box office charts.

THE NEW INTENSITY

Jaws, *Close Encounters of the Third Kind* and *Raiders of the Lost Ark* established new standards for thrill and awe. In conjunction with those of other filmmakers, these efforts by Steven Spielberg changed the movie industry, restoring its central position in American popular culture. His stories and thrill-seeking style matched the shifts in the American political climate that resulted in Ronald Reagan's election in the 1980s. But the academic and critical rush to judgment that his stories presented a right-wing vision was too quick.[11] There was a detectable skepticism about American institutions in the tension between the sheriff and the mayor in

Jaws, the skirmishes between Roy Neary and the American army, the military hysteria in *1941*, but it must be admitted that Spielberg constructed the films so that the audiences could ignore these elements. Stories of engaged struggle were not important compared to the premium pleasures of thrills, awe, and action.

The main characters of these movies often act as surrogates for the audience, and their attitudes are necessarily middling and unchallenging. Ironically, the characters in these films are often tepid, since the hip factor is provided by the visual pyrotechnics. It is natural that by the end of this period, Spielberg has a new level of confidence in his film language. This was important in foreshadowing a shift in Spielberg's own ambition. Filmmaking craft is an education in how to tell a story. Eventually a sincere interest in the craft also prods the filmmaker to think about why she or he wants to tell a story. Spielberg had fulfilled his overwhelming ambition to please a massive audience. He now becomes more open to telling his own stories. His biographer, Joseph McBride, argues that the key to the dawning of Spielberg's cinematic ambition is his friendship with Steven Ross, the CEO of Warner Communications, starting in 1981. Ross was the older man and of course had a professional interest in getting the younger man to direct films for Warner. The relationship helped develop the filmmaker's interest in different kinds of artistic expressions (McBride, 382–83). Nonetheless the filmmaker never gave up his obsession with pleasing the audience. Even his personal stories were destined to be expressions of mass culture.

4

E.T. AND ALL THINGS PRIVATE

The early Reagan years were a time of anxiety over an economic recession. Interest rates were going up and unemploy-
ment was still relatively high. The people had elected the new
president because of his power to assuage, to offer comforting
solutions for complex problems. His rhetoric played to a
general loss of faith in collective institutions. For instance,
these were bad years for labor unions. Workers lost power
and job situations deteriorated. Decreasing earning power
was one factor motivating both parents to seek paying jobs
outside the home. This caused concern about the family. The
paradoxical result of the economic anxiety was thus a turn
away in media discourses from the macro worlds of business
and politics, to focus instead on private things. In general-
interest magazines, newspapers, and TV shows, the most
relevant example was the number of stories about increased
pressure on marriages; on divorce; and on latchkey children.

During the shooting of *Raiders of the Lost Ark*, Spielberg
was thinking about stories influenced by his own childhood

experiences. He described to Melissa Mathieson an idea about a boy becoming friends with an alien from outer space. She wrote out the script about this friendship and it went into production. It was the final feature film that the filmmaker was obliged to make for Universal under his original contract and the budget and scale of production were smaller than his recent films. *E.T., the Extra-Terrestrial* was released in the summer of 1982. Week after week, stretching into three months, huge numbers came to the theaters to make this the most popular film of his career to date. This time the formula was not driven by spectacular costly effects but by a small sentimental story. Even twenty years later, Spielberg affirms that out of his long career, this movie continues to be the closest to his heart. The wish fulfillment of a little boy for a secret companion could have seemed contrived but actually was a genuine expression of the filmmaker's view of life. The *E.T.* script, about a lonely child in a failed marriage, was yet another heartfelt coincidence with the zeitgeist. Steven Spielberg had stumbled upon a popular intersection between his own background as a child of a divorced couple and the socio-political world.

After establishing that an outer space alien (E.T.) has been abandoned by the alien spacecraft in the California forest, the movie cuts to a pizza party in a suburban house, where ten-year-old Elliot (Henry Thomas) lives with his mother (Dee Wallace), older brother (Robert MacNaughton), and younger sister (Drew Barrymore). His absent father has left the family, with a new girlfriend, for Mexico. Elliot is having a hard time fitting in with his brother's friends. He and his mother are suffering from the isolation of the suburbs. Their surroundings are too homogeneous for them to meet the new people they need to meet. In contrast, the older brother fits in while the sister is too young to feel the constrictions of cul-de-sac developments.

As Elliot wanders off on his own, he discovers the extra-
terrestrial hiding in the shed. The rest of the movie depicts
his attempts to share his life with E.T. At first he hides the
alien from everyone and then he brings his brother and sister
into the secret. E.T. starts to learn to communicate and
demonstrates some of his superior powers to heal living
things and to transmit emotions telepathically. Government
agents are in the area, presumably looking for signs of alien
life. When E.T. falls sick, the children cannot hide him
anymore and the government moves in to sequester the
house. The movie is resolved when E.T. revives (is resur-
rected?). The children take advantage of the distracted adults
to run off with a living E.T. to a rendezvous in the forest
where the spaceship comes back to pick up the alien.

Technically, Spielberg worked in a more open style. This
was the first time he did not storyboard the film. (Storyboarding is the process of drawing the various shots planned for the
movie on paper, in order to prepare for the production.) While
a few directors disdain such elaborate pre-planning, the young
Spielberg, emulating Alfred Hitchcock and other masters of
suspense, did meticulous storyboards. In television it was part
of his political strategy to convince the producers to support
complex visualizations and it became an intrinsic part of his
thrill-seeking style. Therefore when he announced that he was
not using storyboard, he was telling the viewers to watch the
film in a different way; to be open to improvisations in the
service of character development. He wants to move beyond
the craft of pre-conceived imagery for the sake of freshness.
After *E.T.*, he would announce from time to time that he
avoided storyboarding, notably for *Schindler's List*. This always
signified that Spielberg wanted the film to be viewed as more
humanistic than spectacular or thrill-seeking.

Despite this openness there was a strong predetermination
in the framing. In this movie, Spielberg plunges the viewers

into Elliot's world. Scene after scene was shot from three feet off the ground to represent the point of view of the boy and/ or the alien. Adults were cut off by this angle. The government agents traipsing through the woods were mostly shown from the waist down; the most prominent one had a bunch of keys hanging on his belt. Although this agent (Peter Coyote) became an important part of the movie's ending, he never was named and was listed only as "Keys" in final credits. Elliot introduced E.T. (and us) to his action toys, and the movie kept returning to the closet full of stuffed dolls as a respite from the hostile world. The camera gave more respect to toys and other objects important to a child, rather than to adult things.

E.T. was carefully conceived to be a soft creature from another world whose actual height and disadvantaged position on earth mirrored Elliot's own sense of frustration. Great care was taken to create E.T. as a soft, fleshy figure; neither eco-skeletal nor with the ghostlike features that had been used before in alien representations. To be sure the alien was not cuddly, and several have commented that E.T. was designed to be ugly and to resemble a frog (Gordon, 77–78). Thus, with great skill, the visualization of E.T. referred to a long tradition of fairy tales and folk stories finding human mirrors in the animal kingdom. But it was a tradition that is specifically filtered through the prewar work of the Disney studios for the moviegoers. They associated E.T. with the soft figures of the seven dwarfs in *Snow White and the Seven Dwarfs* (1937) and other Disney creations. Spielberg, himself, referred to many things Disney, such as *Fantasia* (1940), when explaining the night scenes (Gordon, 81).

Thus media writers (and presumably the audience) naturally compare Spielberg to Disney. But that apt comparison overlooks a subtle and vital difference. Robin Wood, who is otherwise a skeptical critic of sentimental filmmaking, is subtle enough to realize that Spielberg is much less calculating than the Disney team (1990, 294). This lack of calculation can be immediately evidenced by Spielberg's willingness to represent the dystopia of contemporary American life. Unlike the postwar Disney, Spielberg's writers were not burdened by a need to celebrate in the face of a communist threat. Indeed, if they had painted too much of a white-picket-fence picture of Americana, they would have given up the "hip" aspect of the contemporary blockbuster code.

Certainly Disney would never have allowed US government agents to be the heavies. But in this film they become the space invaders in a particularly creepy scene when they penetrate Elliot's home through the doors, the garage, and even the windows in full moon-walking space suits. The flag patches on their suits do not reassure the audience. Instead the staging of the home invasion fulfilled a generational belief that American agents are intrusive and incompetent. The only time the government scientists reveal their faces is when they suppose that E.T. is dead. This is not Disneyland, where an authority figure may be a comic bungler but never a masked invader.

While *Close Encounters* depicted a dystopia, *E.T.* passively assumed a background malaise. It is interesting that while the suburbs in *Close Encounters* were Midwestern, Spielberg places *E.T.* unambiguously in the sunbelt, by combining locations from southern and northern California. Disney's suburbia and other depictions, even through the 1970s, were generally of the same ambience as Norman Rockwell's generic white-picket-fence towns that could belong anywhere in America.[12] *E.T.* is quite specific to the barren tracts of California. Ground cover and foliage can only be maintained by irrigation and are quite absent in one scene of a bicycle chase through lots still being built. The rhythms of the

On the left is an actual sunbelt suburb and above is the location for the action in E.T. *Spielberg finally captures his youth on film.*

neighborhood are similarly barren. Most of the time there is no one on the streets of the cul de sac on which Elliot's family lives. This is the opposite of a vibrant town sidewalk (as portrayed in any number of 1960s comedies) where people come and go for a variety of reasons throughout the day until finally things settle for the night. No variety or randomness is seen on Elliot's street. The few times there are people they are there for a single purpose: kids waiting for the school bus, or the curious gawking at the police surrounding Elliot's house. It is almost redundant that they want to isolate the house since it is already isolated when we first see it at night. The house is perched on a rise and emits lights (a pattern of lights we saw earlier with the spacecraft), which visually confirms that it is not rooted, that the house could rise and fly off into space.

The most overt portrayal of the malaise is the loneliness of Elliot's mother. She cannot see E.T. even when she is in the same room with the alien. We do not see her able to interact with anyone else beside her children and even there the interaction is quite limited by her frantic schedule and misunderstandings of their relationships. Even her sexual frustration is expressed in an open way when she dresses up for Halloween. Although Spielberg's motives were saccharine, he did not sugarcoat the undermining of parental authority in a broken marriage. The mother's inadequacy is a touch that Spielberg shares with the older part of his "all-age" audience.

But the movie does not force the audience to be interested in grown-up emotions or to dwell on the consequences of divorce. Elliot's situation is more universal than that of a child in a divorce. The divorce, and the sunbelt malaise, even the dubious realism of a lily-white cast (one African-American policeman was the lone exception) were ignored by the mass audience seeking to indulge their own wish fulfillment. The audience used the movie to feel reassured even as lifestyles were changing. The nuclear family of the 1950s was going sub-nuclear. Not even couples were staying together, let alone extended families or communities. Spielberg's artistic response was to tell a story of comfort. This impulse becomes obvious when one considers how little the story demands of Elliot and how little the film demands of the audience. Elliot does not have to "deserve" E.T. and he does not have to master a life lesson in order to save the alien. Indeed E.T. has little to teach him. The alien's telepathic abilities are magical without any pretense that they are the result of advanced science or another rational explanation.

This can be contrasted with any number of classical Hollywood stories of lonely boys finding surrogate fathers and/or companions. Spielberg reports that one of his own favorites from the early period was Victor Fleming's *Captains Courageous* (1937). In this movie, a rich boy (Frederick Bartholomew), being raised by a single parent, falls overboard en route to Europe and is retrieved from the sea by a fisherman named Manuel (Spencer Tracy). He learns lessons about hard work and standing up for what is right when circumstances force him to stay with the fishing boat for its entire cruise. These are real life passages, not feel-good empathies. Even the parting is hard-edged, since the boy must watch as Manuel dies while saving the ship. In contrast, Spielberg reached the highest plateau of popularity by instinctively softening the hard life lessons of earlier times in favor of wish fulfillment.

This parallels how Spielberg soft-pedaled the "enemy of the people" angle in *Jaws*, government duplicity in *Close Encounters*, and the satire of American capacity for hysteria in *1941*. Like the other films, the softness of *E.T.* brought in the massive audience. His blockbuster formula of hinting at failure in American life and yet not asking his audience to really look at this failure worked again. It should be noted how far he had gone in accepting his generation's negative feeling about authority; eventually, though, he pulled his punch. The script refrained from portraying government officials as causing any fatal damage (E.T. was already ill before they intervened). "Keys," the government agent, expressed sympathy for Elliot. Spielberg never quite portrayed the government as the enemy, even if the agents were obstacles.

It was a new plateau in profitable popularity. Again Spielberg was invited to Reagan's White House to show the hottest movie of the season. Again the box office surpassed all records (except that of *Star Wars*). But *E.T.* also pioneered new markets to become an emblem of cross-media marketing in early 1980s Hollywood. In just one of many deals, Atari paid Universal $21 million to create a video game based on the film (*Variety* December 15, 1982).[13] The merchandising of products based on the movie earned revenues for both Spielberg and Universal that exceeded what the film itself earned. There may have been $1 billion gross sales on the tie-ins (Morris, 84–85) while the initial release of the film sold $701 million tickets worldwide. Universal soon released the film again in 1985 for another $40 million.

Despite or because of all the earnings, Spielberg resisted one opportunity in an emerging market. By 1982 pre-recorded video had started to return significant revenue to the major studios. Goldman Sachs estimates that it accounted for 10 percent of the $3.5 billion movies earned in that year. Three of Spielberg's movies had been released to video at that time (*Close Encounters*, *Jaws*, and *1941*) and all three had sold more than one million dollars' worth each and thus placed near the top ten for their categories. The director was not particularly keen to see his movies on video, however. "I'm not crazy about [video], and I know what went into [the movie] . . . four years of my life, and I can hold it in one hand without my hand getting tired . . . there's something about that that bothers me. I think what I am trying to say is that I believe in showmanship." Nonetheless, Spielberg played it both ways. He refused to allow a video release of *E.T.*, and he also contracted for 50 percent of the revenues if there was a video release (Sanello, 111–12). By 1986 video revenue matched theatrical revenue (Wasser, 2001, 153). In 1988 Spielberg finally allowed *E.T.* on video and it sold 10 to 12 million units allowing Universal and Spielberg to split almost $160 million. It was sold at the relatively low price of $30 so that people could own it rather than rent it.

STEVEN SPIELBERG IS NOW SPIELBERG

The great popularity of *E.T.* propelled the director to even more exalted heights of mass culture. It is with this film that Steven Spielberg becomes Spielberg. He not only has full control of his career but he has the power to launch other directors on their own careers. After *E.T.*, Spielberg continued to expand his activities as a producer, particularly on *Poltergeist* (1982). Many label it a Spielberg movie although the director was Tobe Hooper. There were many more alliances; the most famous of this time period were with Joe Dante and Robert Zemeckis. In particular, Zemeckis's imagination closely paralleled that of Spielberg and for a while his filmmaking is practically an extension of his mentor's work. In 1985, Spielberg produced *Back to the Future*, a movie that was directed by Zemeckis. It would be the top earner for the year, reaching ticket sales that almost equaled the master's best efforts.

THE BACKLASH

As movies regained popular prominence in the aftermath of *Jaws* and *Star Wars*, there was a decline in personal explorations by big studio filmmakers. In response, Susan Sontag and other intellectuals complained about the death of cinema. Even Pauline Kael, an early champion of Spielberg, seemed disenchanted by the disappearance of adult themes. She now stated, "Why are movies so bad . . . it comes down to the success of Steven Spielberg" (Blum, 55). The critique was not against Spielberg; it was a lament that serious films had been replaced by the Spielberg school. In the various stories that ranged from children finding pirate's treasure to old timers finding the capacity to still be young, the Spielberg school demanded nothing from their audience and gave them every fantastic wish fulfillment. Since nothing was ever demanded the films "have started to look remarkably, and distressingly, alike . . . about kids, suburbs and middle-class American values" (Blum, 54). The critical assessment of academic other intellectuals in the 1980s was that these stories had little or no weight and that the attraction was merely a matter of spectacle.

There seemed to be few alternatives to the mainstream. The new markets of video and cable undermined the margins for art theaters and cult movie showings. Sleazy albeit subversive movie venues disappeared even from New York City's famed 42nd street. Both art houses and third-run theaters were disappearing. Midnight screenings of cult films faded in the mid-1980s. Exploitation films were released straight-to-video but their cultural significance dropped with the loss of any theatrical exposure. The seedy circuits at one time could have provided a counterweight to Spielbergian mainstreaming but now the new markets were eliminating these venues. It is ironic that even Spielberg resisted video although it was he and not others who pocketed the lion's portion of the new money. It was unfair to blame Spielberg for all these changes, but he had become the dominant vision of Hollywood as Hollywood was driving all other moviemakers out of even the small niches where they still hoped to gather a crowd. It was natural for the critics to see the coincidence between the rise of all things Spielberg and the loss of alternatives.

This period was not kind to Spielberg's cohort. Francis Ford Coppola was hemorrhaging power in 1982 with the flop of *One From the Heart* and the loss of his Los Angeles studio. He made perhaps his finest films in 1983 with his two S. E. Hinton projects, *The Outsiders* and *Rumblefish*, but the audience did not respond to a sufficient degree. He was no longer the force he had been when he helped launch George Lucas in the mid-1970s. Lucas himself had wrapped the last of the first three Star Wars movies in 1983 and was less engaged, although he maintained a very active role as producer and executive producer on many projects. He was very interested in developing sound systems, editing studios, and special effects companies. Hal Ashby had visibly lost his directorial clout when he could not get a studio to properly handle *Second Hand Heart* in 1982. William Friedkin, Arthur Penn, and Peter Bogdanovich had all slowed down. Robert Altman had to reinvent himself as a director of small-budget movies. To some degree this was the natural passing of a generation of creative people in a high-stakes business, but the cycle had been vastly speeded up.

The changing of the guard was occasion for a lowering of the prestige of the film director. The movie studios quickly seized on reports of a more conservative audience to end any flirtation with political expression. Right-wing ideology was now expressed by passivity and the absolute separation of politics from entertainment in the film industry (Ryan and Kellner). Entertainment values were unabashedly dominant. Even the publicity value of the "auteur" eroded. While Spielberg, Lucas, and a few others retained their marketing appeal, the director's name was losing value. The prominent names now emerging in the industry were producers such as Dino DeLaurentiis,[14] Don Simpson, Jerry Bruckheimer, Mario Kassar, and Andrew Vajna. But the audience didn't know these names and they didn't care. The industry had perfected another way of getting the audience to immediately recognize the value of a movie even if they did not know the "auteur's" name.

Movie studios made it known that projects would be approved if they could be easily marketed to a global audience. The buzzword for this criterion was "high concept." High concept was the catch-all phrase for new ways to familiarize and excite the audience about the film even before they saw it. Justin Wyatt has an academic study of these new ways, which he codified as the look, the hook, and the book. His examples run towards the use of music, story lines familiar from other media, and so forth. What was a diminishing part of the mix was the brand name of the director. The emphasis in high concept filmmaking was taken from television: familiarity, or even more to the point, immediate visualization. Spielberg himself provided one of the operative definitions of high concept that floated around the town in the early 1980s when he said, "If a person can tell me the idea in twenty-five words or less, it's going to make a pretty good movie" (Wyatt, 13).

High concept was not just an autonomous development but was part of a general acceleration of consumerist life in the 1980s. The call for quickly summarized story lines came from television, where the short blurbs in *TV Guide* were the primary means to lure viewers for that evening's program. Thus former TV executives such as Barry Diller and Michael Eisner had no problems when they moved to the film world to demand stories that could also be summarized in a short compelling blurb. While we accept that high concept itself was vague, its pernicious effect on the movies was captured by Tom Shone: "these films that had been shorn of peripherals, strip-mined for their pockets of triumph, their character arcs reduced to telegraphic shorthand, and strung out along a gleaming bead of hit songs—that's what high concept was, or felt like to watch" (176).

Every filmmaker must be a businessman, particularly in the age of cross-media marketing. In 1981 Paramount launched a daily television show called *Entertainment Tonight*, featuring the comings and goings of celebrities as if this was "news." The pressure was on successful directors to publicize themselves more as celebrity business leaders than as autonomous artists. On a broader scale everyone was being forced to be a freelancer, to take more responsibility and risks in relationship to their careers. Corporations were dissolving the old Fordist contract between labor and capital, which exchanged a certain expectation of security for a level of loyalty. Careerism had always been rampant in show business; surprisingly, there was room for it to go to a higher level than ever before.

Another unfortunate coincidence was between the political swing to marketplace capitalism and the mainstreaming of film. The entire society had shifted its primary goal from production to sales and this was precisely the mantra of Hollywood. The studios actually decreased production during the mid-1980s in order to spend more money on marketing. While the raw data was ambiguous from year to year, a pattern emerges if we take five-year averages. The averages kept declining approximately by 10 percent from the mid-1970s to 1992. There were 512 major releases in 1974 and only 276 in 1992. A better and less dramatic statistic was looking at the MPAA releases, without counting independent releases. They decline up through 1981, increase slightly through 1987, decline again until 1992. There were only 129 releases in 1987 after a high point of 190 in 1983. The strategy worked; MPAA revenues went up every year through the 1980s and early 1990s. Increased revenue was not used for more production; it was used for more marketing.

Spielberg was aware that his name signified a certain high concept all by itself. He continually originated ideas that were easy to describe, and once described the resulting movies were easy to visualize and thus easy to market. The challenge in making such high concept films was to hold the viewer's attention from scene to scene, since the frailties of such films are their overly obvious banalities. After *E.T.*, he continued to generate such story ideas, but now he farmed them out to other directors. This contributed to the impression that his ideas were everywhere while other voices were disappearing.

A Setback and a Disappointment

Although generally Spielberg could handle the pressures of
the artist/businessman connection, the 1983/84 cycle led to
a crisis in producing and a disappointment in filmmaking.
The crisis occurred when he arranged to make a compilation
film based on the television show *The Twilight Zone* (CBS,
1959–1964). The gimmick was to have four directors to film
four different stories to go together into one film. Spielberg's
team was producing and providing overall coordination.
They were in a position of responsibility when one of the
directors, John Landis, flagrantly defied legal restrictions
regarding the use of underage actors. During his night shoot,
a helicopter crashed and killed two children and the veteran
actor Vic Morrow. In the ensuing disciplinary actions and
court cases, Spielberg was never held responsible.

The accident itself was a sign of the times. The unsafe
conditions were created by a management team dedicated to
getting the exciting shot at any cost, the consequence of the
new blockbuster formula. The team was working with a
cowed labor force unwilling to stand up to the director. This
resonated with a dominant ideology that disdained regulations as mere obstacles. Even though Landis was fined and
censured, he was acquitted of the most severe charge by a
jury who seemed easily impressed by his high position in
society. Landis continued his career as a big-budget filmmaker (although his relationship with Spielberg ceased).
Spielberg made few public comments, although critics
thought they could detect chagrin in the perfunctory manner
with which he finished his directoral and production duties
on the ill-fated film.

In general, Hollywood was becoming more ruthless and
hard-edged. Three movies had come out in 1982 that did not
reach the top ten in box office but would prove to have an

enduring influence, expressing the braggadocio of the growing right wing. *Blade Runner* starred Harrison Ford of the Indiana Jones series but used him as a much more violent and unforgiving hero. *Conan the Barbarian* launched the career of Arnold Schwarzenegger as an extreme killer. But it was *Rambo: First Blood* that most fully captured the intersection between popular culture and emerging themes of Republican backlash against the left-wing movements of the 1960s. Rambo (Sylvester Stallone) had been trained by the US Army to kill outside the law in Vietnam. Now he was back in America, his comrades were dead, and he felt scorned by the America that he thought he was defending in Vietnam. The movie becomes a compelling tale of violent survival and destruction. Within a few years and with an even more successful sequel, it would become a sign of the times.

Spielberg's next solo directing assignment was *Indiana Jones and the Temple of Doom* (1984). This was when he made his closest approach to the retrogressive ideologies of the era, because he was willing to include more violence and other vicarious thrills at the expense of the narrative. Work on scripting *Indiana Jones and the Temple of Doom* began soon after *Raiders of the Lost Ark*. The script recycled many of the discarded ideas from the first film, but despite the continuities the film had a different mood, within the same general frame of matinee-inspired action/adventure. Literally the tone changed, since the film begins with an extended nightclub scene, while the entire second act and most of the final part takes place in the darkness of the temple and of the underground mine. The recycling of old Hollywood seemed more indulgent and less unified than the first film. There was an extended Busby Berkeley-like dance number, the nightclub referenced old detective movies (such as the Charlie Chan series), and many parts were inspired by the colonial iconography of *Gunga Din* (1939). The screwball flirtations between Indiana Jones (Harrison Ford) and Willie Scott (Kate Capshaw) lacked sizzle because of Spielberg's famous lack of adroitness with sex scenes and because they were planted in a boyish adventure. The genre blending became an unwieldy mélange.

The filmmaking followed *Raiders'* formula of nonstop "you have never seen this before" action. Everything was goosed. The film took advantage of the latest surround-sound theater systems to use sound effects to amplify the dimensionality of the action. For example, at one point the central focus of the story was a loose capsule that contained the antidote Indiana needed. The sound of that little pill capsule rolling around on the floor as the crowd went to and fro in the club was heightened to the point of parody. Another showstopper was the literal roller coaster ride when the bad guys chase the good guys on mining carts rolling down the tracks at faster and faster speeds. Spielberg fully utilized the opportunities to put the camera in the carts and to give the audience the exhilaration of out-of-control speed.

The film was rewarded with a profitable audience but for a Spielberg project it drew an unusual amount of criticism and complaints. The filmmakers should have realized the extent of their racial insensitivity when the Government of India refused to let them work in Rajasthan (Freer, 137). Most of the effective complaints concerned the graphic violence. Lucas and Spielberg definitely wanted a young audience and used many young actors. There was Indiana Jones' ten-year-old sidekick Short Round (Ke Huy Quan), a young Indian prince, and many enslaved children. The immersive techniques also targeted a thrill-seeking young audience. The two men judged that today's children needed the extra buzz of absurdly fast-paced action and shocking imagery. In one scene guests had to eat from monkey heads and were served soup with intact eyeballs in the middle of the broth. Even more disturbing was the brutality of the various fights. A hypnotized Indiana Jones comes dangerously close to destroying his female companion. The most egregious scene was when Mola Ram (Amrish Puri) pulled a human heart out of the victim's chest on camera. Foreign censors cut various scenes. In the US the MPAA ratings board talked of giving the film a "R" rating, which would have obliged theater owners to turn away young children. However, Spielberg used his clout to get the PG rating, which allowed children to see it although parents had been warned that some scenes were not suitable.

Some critics explained that both Lucas and Spielberg were going through rough personal patches. But I wish to make a more speculative argument. The two creators of the Raiders series had an almost effortless ability to understand and cater to a mass audience. By this time in the mid-1980s they had sensed the further coarsening of audience taste. It is always hard to detect trends in the movies but the growth of home video had inspired a wave of gory, violent productions that the British press had labeled "nasties." There had been a noticeable uptick of horror and slasher movies. *Halloween* made its debut in 1978, *Friday the 13th* in 1980 and *Nightmare on Elm Street* in 1984. All three titles would continue to spawn sequels for the next two decades. Despite their R (restricted) ratings, their audiences overlapped with the Raiders audience.

The television shows of those years were also becoming more explicit about sex, violence, and general belligerence. *Hill Street Blues* (NBC 1981–1987) had pushed the gritty realism of the police precinct to new heights. On that show Spielberg's former collaborator on *Columbo*, Steven Bochco, was a leading force in writing into the script explicit references to sexual desire and using street language right up to and over the decency limit set by the government. Indeed, the Federal Communications Commission seemed less concerned, and cost-conscious networks started to cut down on their standards-and-practices staff. One result was *The A-Team* (NBC, 1983–1987), a prime-time program that was notorious for its aggressive language and high rate of inconsequential violence. Violence had always been present in movies and television but there was increased pressure to escalate it during the 1980s as the two media became more competitive.

Thus *Temple of Doom* actually mirrored and anticipated the rise of coarse imagery in popular culture. The floodgates were opening as the Reagan administration continued a policy of deregulation that allowed more freedom on television. There was a right-wing belief that the market was better at solving problems than the government. Therefore conservative politicians had little to say about the rise of violence and sexual innuendo that were succeeding in mainstream markets such as network television while they denounced explicit sex in a marginalized pornography industry. It may seem contradictory, but by the mid-1980s the trend was to have more TV titillation and violence, with producers and regulators alike knowing full well that children would be watching. Lucas/Spielberg were correct in assuming that children had seen more and were attracted to stronger images than previous generations.

Nonetheless, after the May 1984 release, Spielberg grew to regret the film. The first action he took was to argue successfully for an intermediate rating—PG-13—that would suggest more forcefully to parents that the film was rather strong. Many years later Spielberg admitted that "I wasn't happy with [*Temple of Doom*] at all. It was too dark, too subterranean and much too horrific. I thought it out-poltered *Poltergeist*. There's not an ounce of my own personal feeling in *Temple of Doom*" (McBride, 355).

No More Action

From *Temple of Doom* in 1984 until *Indiana Jones and the Last Crusade* in 1989, Spielberg did not make another action feature film. Perhaps the success of *E.T.* reassured him that he did not have to do action, that he had the skills to make films about family dramas. He didn't need a middling-bland hero such as David Mann (*Duel*) or Sheriff Brody (*Jaws*) to pull the audience into a thrill ride. *E.T.* had worked on other emotions and pleasures. These five years were a time of a cultural hardening in America. The first period of the Reagan administration was full of rhetorical change and incremental policy shifts. Now the incremental was starting to make a real difference to the landscape of America. The rise in the unequal distribution of income was starting; poverty was more visible, as well as wealth. Only the middle class seemed to be disappearing.

It would take a period of exploration as a film director before Spielberg would discover once again where his personal feelings and his audience intersected. In this gap between the two Indiana Jones projects, he turned to the historical past for a string of projects. Big-budget historical filmmaking had largely disappeared with the end of the road show era in the mid-1960s. Twenty years later it was starting to reappear (albeit with smaller budgets), in a meaningful effort to counterprogram films against the dominance of action. British filmmakers gained some American attention with modest films targeted at an audience that was interested in literature and cultural heritage. In the early 1980s an English company, Goldcrest Ltd., conceived the ambition to serve a niche market of audiences who still loved the historic films of the 1960s. The results on both sides of the Atlantic were initially positive as the company did well with *Chariots of Fire* (1981) and its co-production of *Gandhi* (1982). Both films won the Oscar for best picture. Another even smaller production company, Merchant/Ivory, was also slowly building itself up by making literary films, often set in the nineteenth century. In 1985 Goldcrest and Merchant/Ivory cooperated on a film adaptation of E. M. Forster's *Room With A View*. This broke out of the campus movie circuit to earn a highly respectable $20 million at the American box office. The two companies were leaders in identifying a trans-Atlantic audience for literary and historic projects, the so-called heritage films. This caught the attention of several big studios as well as Spielberg.

In 1982, Universal had bought the rights to Thomas Kenneally's *Schindler's Ark*, a successful novelization of Oskar Schindler's activities during the German occupation of Poland. Sid Sheinberg was already thinking of Spielberg for the film. But the filmmaker hesitated and would spend ten years elsewhere before embarking on this story of the Holocaust. Still, this was a period of transition when he was turning his attention to foreign stories, even as Hollywood was increasing its revenues from foreign audiences. From 1985 to 1990 the percentage of money the American film industry earned from overseas increased from 23 percent to 39 percent. By 1995 it was 51 percent (Wasser, 2002, 356). Spielberg movies would lead this trend. All his big money-makers through *E.T.* (1982) made the majority of their money in the domestic market. *Close Encounters* was the one exception, with 51 percent foreign earnings in 1978. After *The Color Purple* (1985) all his films earned a higher percentage overseas except for *Always* (1989) and *Amistad* (1997).

This unremarked trend is indicative of the greater power of US distributors in Europe and Asia, but the fact that Spielberg should be in the forefront suggests that he was rethinking his audience. He will still tell stories of hope and triumph, but the overly obvious wish-fulfillment aspect would fall away a stick figure, since his character was an ineffective mélange of real historic figures. Historical inaccuracy was not the only problem. The film's reception suffered from a plagiarism suit, which was eventually dropped. Spielberg drew his own lesson: "I kind of dried it out and it became too much of a history lesson" (Freer, 258). He moved on to his World War Two epic.

THE CONTEXT OF *SAVING PRIVATE RYAN*

1994 was fifty years after the D-Day invasion. While Hollywood missed the boat on timing a film to the event, the historian Stephen Ambrose had coordinated the publication of his collection of ordinary soldiers' memories with the anniversary. The book recounts the story of the Niland brothers, three of whom died in combat. This, and a local monument, inspired an up-and-coming screenwriter, Robert Rodat, to script the fictional story *Saving Private Ryan*, which was bought by Paramount and shown by them to Steven Spielberg and Tom Hanks. Both committed to the historical fiction combat film in early 1996 (Fleming). There had not been a major American World War Two film since the 1970s.[25]

The director, writers, actors, and other parties reported motivations for *Private Ryan* that ranged from abstract thoughts about war and duty, specific thoughts about World War Two and the Vietnam War, and the new category of generational memories. We can also consider Spielberg's desire to add to the Hollywood legacy by recycling one of its hallowed genres, the war movie. No artistic motivation is purely nostalgic, especially when engaged with history. In this case there is not only one context for the launching of the film, there are three: political, generational, and cinematic.

The Clinton administration had a more inclusive view of America's relationship with the world than its predecessors. Meanwhile, a conservative response to the fall of communism was to move America into greater isolation and obstruct President Clinton's inclinations to intervene in foreign trouble spots. General Colin Powell promoted a doctrine that limited military invention to situations where deployment of overwhelming force would minimize American casualties. Correspondingly in the 1990s there was military reluctance to go to trouble spots. After a disastrous October 1993 fire-fight in Somalia, Clinton quickly withdrew American soldiers from that conflict. There was no consideration in 1994 of using the US military to stop genocide in Rwanda. Clinton did have some success in stabilizing Haiti with the Marines in that same year. But the Pentagon's attitude towards inter-ventions continued to be hesitant, despite the President's determination to stop ethnic bloodshed in Kosovo.

The Yugoslav wars were the largest military and genocidal actions on the continent of Europe since 1945. Ethnic murder and warfare broke out in 1990, and these events had already given a sense of urgency to the 1993 production of *Schindler's List*. The Bosnia-Croat phase of these wars had wound down by 1995, but the Kosovo phase flared up in 1998, the year *Private Ryan* was released. Europe had failed to stop the bloodshed through a lack of political leadership, and even the United States seemed rather timid about getting involved. When the US did decide to act, it was through a compromise that did not include ground troops. Heavy air strikes against aggressors were used instead. It may have minimized the danger for Americans, but it caused more civilian fatalities.

Yugoslavia summoned up many emotions. Therefore, Spielberg and company wanted to explore an earlier era of shared sacrifice and commitment. He and many of his peers had avoided military duty in Vietnam. Many men of the Vietnam generation felt less than heroic either for serving in a "bad" war or for avoiding service. In 1973 the United States switched from a conscripted army to an all-volunteer force. This was part of the post-Vietnam reduction of the citizen's duty to the country. Spielberg's interest in shared sacrifice came out of a generational feeling of guilt over the Vietnam War.

Confusion and immorality has been true of every war, but the Vietnam generation was the first to force these ambivalences and lapses into the open. Spielberg was determined to go back and make a movie that posed the same questions about World War Two, while at the same time expressing admiration for a generation that fought that earlier war. It was an easy way to flatter an American audience: tell a story about what was to be called the "greatest" generation because the people born in the late 1910s and early 1920s survived the Depression and won the war against Japan and Germany. The generational context leads directly to the cinematic context.

The 1998 film Saving Private Ryan *was a long-overdue revival of the populist spirit of the platoon of citizens working together for the collective nation.*

Saving Private Ryan uses many of the tropes familiar to older viewers from movies such as *A Walk in the Sun* (1945) and *Battleground* (1949), and TV shows such as *Combat* (ABC 1962–1967). They showed teamwork and cooperation among ordinary citizens. Leaders and heroes were not a class apart but were of the same background as their men. The one common omission was any reference to the segregation of the armed forces (although in *Battleground* there was a minimal effort to show nonwhite personnel). The war movie took a different course during the 1980s. Hollywood used themes of disintegration, leadership dysfunction, and personal crises when it finally started to release films such as *The Deer Hunter* (1978), *Apocalypse Now* (1979), *Rambo: First Blood* (1982), and *Platoon* (1986). Media depictions of the integrating World War Two platoons are in contrast with depictions of the disintegrating Vietnam-era soldier. An equally popular strain of war films featured somewhat more fantastic heroes. Sylvester Stallone (the Rambo series), Arnold Schwarzenegger (*Commando*, 1985), and Chuck Norris (*Missing In Action*, 1985) played self-reliant veterans who pioneered the genre known as the "Army of One" films. Their characters rarely had helpers and if they started out with friends, these friends were often dead by the middle of the movie. Cooperation and teamwork was minimized to feature a single hero's capabilities. These films have been discussed as part of the male rampage cycle.

ENCOMPASSING THE WAR: *SAVING PRIVATE RYAN*

In order to demonstrate the multiple determinations of *Saving Private Ryan*, the director frames the World War Two story with a present-day scene of an old man and three generations of his presumed family visiting a gravesite in

non violenv
expectancy theory)

Normandy. The American flag gets its own close-up as the group tours the headstones and the old man breaks down in tears at the sight of one of the names. There is a sound overlap and the picture cuts to the 1944 D-Day invasion, shot with a hand-held camera. In the chaos of the landing, where men are being maimed and killed on screen and on the edge of the screen, the camera finally directs the audience's attention to Captain Miller (Tom Hanks). As the carnage becomes overwhelming we realize that we are experiencing it as he experiences it. The sound goes silent when he has a momentary breakdown. The sound comes back up as he regains initiative and leads his men in a successful attack on a German bunker. The invasion scene ends with a masterful release for the audience: the screen opens up to a full shot of the entire beach overrun by the US army.

In Washington, DC, a female clerk realizes that three out of four Ryan brothers have been killed in action. General Marshall (Harve Presnell) orders that the fourth brother be pulled out of the line and sent to safety for the duration of the war. Back on the front no one knows where the fourth brother is and Captain Miller is assigned a platoon to find him. The team of eight men set off and immediately lose a man in a confusing firefight in a bombed-out town. There are further encounters, both with tattered units of the US Army and with occasional German holdouts. The squad almost mutinies after Captain Miller reluctantly stops his men from killing a surrendering German. Miller finally manages to regain control of the unit when he distracts the soldiers by revealing his own civilian background as a schoolteacher.

The depleted squad finds Ryan (Matt Damon) with a ragtag unit holding a key bridge and facing an imminent counterattack from a German tank squad. Ryan refuses to leave his post and Miller decides to stay to help, although he knows the Americans are outnumbered and face long odds. The attack comes and the entire squad is wiped out, although they manage to destroy the tank and to hold on until the US Army Air Force sends in a strike that defeats the Germans. Ryan has survived, and as he administers help to Miller, the dying man tells him to "earn this."

The movie cuts back to the old man and his family by the Normandy gravesite and the elderly Ryan asks his wife whether he has earned it; whether he has led the worthy life. Her affirmative answer fades away as the camera rediscovers the American flag as the final coda.

This time Spielberg did not dry out the history. Color, sound, and the use of the camera did not try to present the viewer with the objective realism of the scene but flattered the viewer by confirming her or his shared memory of World War Two. For example, this time the camera team did not commit to either black-and-white or color but went straight down the middle by using the technique known as bleach bypass, which allowed the team to dial out the color in post-production. The result was a desaturated color image that had the flavor of black-and-white. In terms of realism this process was an admittedly effective balance between the actual reality of the historical past and our memory of it. Janusz Kaminski (encoring his role as Spielberg's director of photography) wanted to desaturate the colors to fit the somber experience, while enhancing the shock value of the red blood. The result was the first combat film to be neither color nor black-and-white.

The most talked-about scene in *Saving Private Ryan* was the first twenty minutes depicting the Omaha Beach invasion. It was designed to make the viewer feel that he or she was in the middle of the landing, and many testified that it did. The scene was perhaps the culmination of Spielberg's career, finally fulfilling his childhood dream of using the camera in

The desaturated color and the randomness of death immerses the viewer of Saving Private Ryan *in D-Day.*

a visceral manner that he could only glimpse in the classic cinema that he had seen on television. The effect was accomplished through the variety of techniques he had picked up thoughout his long career. There were shaky and narrow-perspective hand-held camera shots and images of chaotic action and jerky movements. The explosions hit the audience with visual and acoustic force. Explosions took full advantage of the multiple soundtracks. The placements of the explosions were random, and unnerved the audience, confounding the usual expectation that explosions would either be featured in the center of the frame or placed far in the background. The improvised hand-held work denied the viewer the illusion that any space was safe. The gore was also shocking in that it spared the viewer nothing. Even in the remote corner of the screen a man was getting his limb blown off. The worst mutilations of the human body happened in any place.

Spielberg's audience is less likely than an older generation to have the real experience of war and therefore will tolerate the extreme graphic representation of violence. In any case ne gore fits the expectations of filmgoers today. The horrible images recruit us directly into the American Army. "La place du spectateur est celle du soldat inconnu, de 'l'homme invisible'" (Tesson, 61). For a moment, we become the unknown soldier! For the first few minutes, we are on our own struggling against the German barrage. Only slowly does the camera discover Captain Miller and direct our attention to his problems. Thus the viewer becomes mentally prepared for the mission.

The opening D-Day sequence was praised as one of the great sequences of modern filmmaking. The publicity machine emphasized the enhanced "realism" of *Private Ryan* and asked veterans of the invasion to testify to the "truth" of the opening sequence. The "truth" of this realism is only emotional; there is no corresponding rational truth about the "good" war. Earlier war films just assumed the mutual loyalty of a citizenry. Spielberg's audience has lost faith in national projects and needs more personal reasons as to why one should die for country. Therefore the writers and producers of the film ask us to believe that the mission was not about fighting the Germans. They come dangerously close to defining democracy as the freedom for one man to go home again to his family. Tom Hanks sincerely delivers this most improbable dying line—"James, earn this, earn it!" to Matt Damon. The audience sincerely believes this final admonition to a single person. Private Ryan grows up to provide a happy ending to the war and the movie. His happy life becomes the wish fulfillment. But such individual satisfaction replaces the collective project of building a nation and allows Spielberg to finesse the fault lines of post-Vietnam American politics.

This finesse supports the successful export of the film, since it becomes an open text that can please audiences around the world with their own histories. Ulf Hedetoft studied a variety of global responses to *Saving Private Ryan's* moral, conditioned by positions vis-à-vis America-ness. The French critics see the movie as overtly patriotic and therefore dismiss "Spielberg as a professional manipulator of images and emotions" (101). The Danish critics rather straight-forwardly praise the film's balance between "realism" and "heroism" (103) while the Americans have the most complex position. Critics in the US debate whether Spielberg has raised a soldier's duty to a universal value: "After all, the beneficiary of the anti-heroic heroism of the platoon is Private Ryan (American and Everyman in one), not 'Europe' or 'democratic liberties'" (105).

Private Ryan had instant influence. The TV anchorman Tom Brokaw echoed the spirit of the film in his own 1998 best-selling book The Greatest Generation. Spielberg and Hanks collaborated to produce the TV fiction series Band of Brothers (HBO, 2001). The spirit of Private Ryan was again apparent in Ken Burns's multi-part TV documentary called The War (PBS, 2007). Tom Hanks became involved in the movement to install a World War Two monument on the Capitol Mall. More recently Clint Eastwood made two films about the battle of Iwo Jima that show the visual inspiration of Saving Private Ryan. Spielberg has managed to become the filmmaker who defines World War Two. But in doing so, he exposed a generational fault line that was shared by Brokaw, Burns, Eastwood, and many others. They underplayed the collective New Deal politics that shaped their fathers, and instead created a privatized version of the fight against fascism that was subtly different from the old Hollywood movies.

The platoon movies of the 1940s were still fully invested in the politics of the New Deal and the populism that had become popular in Hollywood in the 1930s during the Depression. This period was a time when Americans looked for an expansion of the public sector in order to protect people from the failures of the marketplace. It was also a time when big business was viewed with suspicion. Hollywood populism was spearheaded by Will Rogers, on the radio and in films, until his accidental death in 1935. Lary May describes moviemakers imagining "America as a place where citizens engaged in self-governing and created a New World republic free of aristocracy and capitalist power." This was a time when "the 'stars' used their celebrity status to promote Labor Day parades and the inclusion of women and minorities in public life" (May, 4).

During World War Two, the platoon films and other movies extolled collective action and people coming together from different walks of life to promote the greater good. Even the romantic individualism of *Casablanca* (1943) was subverted when the lead character Rick Blaine (Humphrey Bogart) provides the moral of the film by saying "that the problems of three little people don't amount to a hill of beans in this crazy world." Because of this political commitment to the collective good, members of the "greatest" generation were the first and primary beneficiaries of the expansion of public services after the war. Their "greatness" was rewarded by the various mass movements that developed the New Deal. Perhaps one of the most important movements in this development was the Bonus March of 1932, setting the stage for veterans' benefits after 1945, which led to the prosperity of the postwar period that lasted through the 1970s. Spielberg's own father took advantage of these benefits.

That sentiment was not sustained in the postwar years, as the very successes of consumer society allowed people to think that collective action was not needed and that market failures were a thing of the past. Private satisfaction increasingly became the only measure of public action. To express this measure, Rodat and Spielberg told a story of a platoon engaged in saving one man and of a Captain Miller who could only imagine that "going home" was the goal for fighting a war. This limited vision of the morality of a generation engaged in total warfare was what Spielberg shared with his audience. He had managed to revive the platoon but not the populism.

THE CENTURY TURNS

Not too long after *Saving Private Ryan*, there were dramatic changes in the relationship between the United States and the world. The political temperature of the United States remained in the conservative zone, despite the efforts of the Democratic administration. President Clinton had some success in implementing foreign policy goals, but the nature of the post-Cold War world was left unsettled, as American partisan bickering obstructed just about every issue. Republicans took control of the Congress in 1994 and successfully stalemated domestic policy initiatives. Organized labor continued to lose ground and families continued the search for more income to maintain a middle-class lifestyle. Welfare payments were decreased. There was an increase in the number of jobs but many Americans still continued to feel a lack of economic security. In 1999 the Republicans staged a surreal albeit failed impeachment proceeding against President Clinton. Nonetheless, they brought George W. Bush to the White House in January 2001. The disputed nature of that election showed that the country was both deeply and evenly split over basic questions of the role of government and the power of corporations.

The partisan tone of the Republicans borrowed heavily from the pop-culture bravado of the Reagan era. Radio shock jocks such as Rush Limbaugh and Don Imus tried mightily to sound like such cinematic aggrieved heroes as Rambo and the Terminator. The 1980s nihilism of Hollywood heroes now permeated the 1990s rhetoric of media pundits and the behavior of political leaders.

However, in a countermovement, the Hollywood film industry had already turned away from its own bravado. Hard-bodied heroes faded away after the turn of the century and the new action films did not closely reflect the unilateral politics. This was because the market was more global than ever. The singular presumption of American virtues was becoming a hard international sell. Instead, more nuanced action heroes, such as Neo of the Matrix series, Spiderman, and the X-Men arose. These action heroes were troubled about their own choices and were considerably less berserk than Sgt. Riggs or Lt. McClane. In this trajectory, Spielberg's turn away from macho action was prescient.

In a world where the blur of appearance and reality had dissolved solidity, the troubled action heroes yearned for the restoration of law, even if they could not bring it back themselves. There was less disdain for public institutions, only regret for their absence. A new narrative, suggested by the maturity of virtual reality technology, dissolved an earlier righteousness that motivated the now fading hard-bodied heroes. The action genre now questioned the objective status of perceived reality. In 1998 and 1999, *Dark City* (dir. Alex Proyas) and *The Matrix* (dirs. Wachowski Brothers) were released. Both feature an untrustworthy relationship between two alternative realities. Both have taken virtual reality at its own premise: that it is indistinguishable from the quotidian real. The characters in *Dark City* are puzzled by their encounters with the other reality, while in *The Matrix* the rebels have largely mastered the programming that controls access in and out of both worlds. The Wachowski brothers combined their reality play with mastery of kung fu acrobatics and even the innovative "bullet-time" shots. The movie grossed over $460

million worldwide, to become the fourth biggest international hit of the year. Its breakthroughs challenged and influenced other big-budget action film directors to also explore
the unreliability of our own senses.

Spielberg was too old-fashioned to question capital-T
Truth, but he was also commissioning scripts about the
digital apocalypse. The next film after *Saving Private Ryan*
was *A.I.: Artificial Intelligence* (2001). The old road school-era
filmmaker Stanley Kubrick had taken a short story about a
robot child programmed to love a real mother and added a
Pinocchio-like journey. The verisimilitude of *Jurassic Park*
inspired Kubrick to involve Spielberg in the development of
the script. Kubrick died in early 1999 and Spielberg decided
to produce and direct the project to honor the older man.
A.I. was released in the summer of 2001 and did a respectable
$236 million in worldwide gross. Its high special-effects
budget limited the profit margin. Unlike *The Matrix*, Spielberg's presentation of the future relies more on mechanical
robots than on digital projections. Therefore it seemed to be
in a genre of one rather than the filmmaker's contribution to
the emerging cycle of futuristic stories. *A.I.* became more of
a cul de sac, rather than a film that really bonded the director
to his audience and times.

Spielberg was now making more of an honest effort to
think about contemporary society than were his blockbusting
buddies. He did not move towards cartoons or fantasy and
turned down an offer to direct the first Harry Potter movie.
Instead, in the late 1990s his company was buying adult projects, such as the novel *Memoirs of A Geisha* and a biography
of Charles Lindbergh. He considered directing these projects
(although he turned over *Memoirs* and seems to have abandoned Lindbergh), which showed his continuing desire to
make historical films. But it is interesting that at Dream-
Works, foreign stories such as *Gladiator* and *Memories* went

to other directors. There is no evidence that Spielberg's team ever consciously targeted a foreign audience.[26] His projects continued to be reflective of an American mentality and explore American dilemmas. *Empire*, *Schindler's List* and *Munich* are possible exceptions, but in each case, the foreign story resonated with specific American interests. Spielberg never shifted cultures; he always presented America to the world.

He was working with established stars to pick projects that re-examined American myths. It is noteworthy that Spielberg, who had made huge hits without stars in the 1970s, now turns to the biggest stars and their massive egos. As far back as 1988 he wanted to direct Dustin Hoffman and Tom Cruise. Although this did not happen until later, he did get Sean Connery in 1989, for the Indiana Jones sequel *The Last Crusade*. Working with stars is not just an expression of maturity for Spielberg, but also of his commitment to an old Hollywood ethos of collaboration.

His next project was *Minority Report*, released nine months after the key date of September 11, 2001. Its reception was conditioned by the terrorist acts.

The dramatic attack on the United States on September 11, 2001, momentarily united the country with the world. But then the American decision to invade Iraq in 2003 ironically isolated the US from its traditional allies and renewed the domestic partisan bickering. Rather quickly the United States became a frightened nation; the constant fear of future attacks has become a significant characteristic of both the political and cultural state. The fear had already been cultivated by a steady stream of movie nihilism of which political leaders took advantage.

The attack also showed the high degree of interconnection between the political and the cultural in the minds of the terrorists. They were motivated by cultural hostility and they planned a high drama that would seize the world's imagination. Their political goals seemed secondary. The ideology of the attackers was not focused on conversion or conquest. The attacks on the towers were done for the sake of gaining prestige within the militant movement of the jihadists. Thus the attacks were motivated only by symbolic aims within a group. This is a stark contrast with traditional aims of national or tribal conquest.

The photogenic power of the World Trade Center (WTC) plane crashes was unmistakable, and led to a momentary gasp from the American audiovisual industry. Media creators wondered if their filmic fantasies had been restaged as true-life horrors (Gabler). American producers had already scripted such attacks and had created a prior close correlation between the fiction and the reality. One example was *The Lone Gunmen* (Fox, 2001). Its pilot episode concerned a plane about to nosedive into one of the twin towers. It aired March 4, six months before the attack. Fox's *24* (2001–2008) was already in pre-production, with a mix of attacks and frantic CIA responses that would serve as the fictional parallel to unfolding events throughout the post-attack period. Movies that featured too many scenes of destruction were pulled from the release schedule. *Spiderman* was famously held up, as its various images of the WTC were removed from the final edit. For the moment, the film industry acted as if images mattered, and wondered with guilt if their digital fictions inspired the deadly Al-Qaeda plot.

DYSTOPIA AND *MINORITY REPORT*

Spielberg's decision to film *Minority Report* was not made in happy times. In 1998 Tom Cruise and Steven Spielberg announced their intention to work together. In this period Cruise sent Spielberg a script for *Minority Report* and both men committed to a 1999 start date. That date failed, as did a 2000 start date. The production finally began in April 2001. We should notice that the various parties committed to the production in the context of the impeachment and the botched recounting of the 2000 election. While *Minority Report* was scripted before actual events caught up to its scenarios, it inadvertently anticipated the preemptive response to the attack by the American government. The Philip K. Dick story, written in 1956, envisioned a world where people were arrested and warehoused for murders they were about to commit. In 2002 the Bush administration announced a policy of attacking countries if these countries might be contemplating hostile actions. They carried out this policy in the 2003 invasion of Iraq. Thus the fictional preemptive crime prevention was an eerie reflection of real preemptive invasions.

The first thing to note is that *Minority Report* is a historical film.[27] Spielberg makes quite certain to establish through titles that the story takes place in the real city of Washington, DC, in the year 2054. This is not the excessive speculation of a science fiction. The humans and the social relations are realistic representations. There are many extrapolations of the present into the future that result in new technology, but each one of these new technologies is already very possible, from retinal scanning to mag-lev vehicles. The only technology that belongs in the realm of the fantastic is the central conceit of mentally damaged humans who can see the truth of future events.

The premise of the film is that Washington, DC, had been plagued by crime and drugs. Three brain-damaged teenagers are discovered to have the ability to foresee future murders with perfect accuracy. A "pre-crime" unit is set up to take advantage of their "pre-cognition" of future murders, and it is legally established that the police can arrest and imprison anyone for the crime of a future murder based on these pre-cognitions. The opening scene shows the unit leader John Anderton (Tom Cruise) assembling images that have been transferred from the consciousness of the "pre-cogs" in order to discover when and who will do the murder. The cops fly out to the scene in their jet packs and catch the perpetrator just before the fatal deed. They place an electronic halo on the would-be killer, which incapacitates him. Since judges were witness to the original pre-cognition, there need not be a trial. The would-be criminal is then warehoused in a zombie-like state in a jail.

John Anderton works under the supervision of the paternal creator of "pre-crime" detention, Lamar Burgess (Max Von Sydow). He is being inspected by FBI agent Danny Witwer (Colin Farrell). In this pressured situation Anderton is astonished to discover that the pre-cogs have visualized his own future act of murder. He flees the police station and escapes a hot pursuit by his fellow cops. He finds out from a retired co-founder of "pre-crime," Iris Hineman (Lois Smith), that the system is not perfect and is therefore motivated to find a dissenting "minority report" in his own case that will clear his name. He kidnaps one of the pre-cogs, Agatha (Samantha Morton), and proceeds to his future murder site. Anderton refuses to kill his intended victim, whereupon the victim commits suicide. Anderton is still on the run when he is captured.

Fortunately his ex-wife learns enough to suspect that he is being set up by Lamar Burgess and engineers his liberation. Burgess had manipulated the system by murdering Agatha's mother Anne Lively (Jessica Harper) several years ago. Anderton now realizes that that is the minority report Agatha wants him to discover. He confronts Burgess and Burgess commits suicide rather than face the consequences of his act. The movie ends with the elimination of the pre-crime

Anderton manipulates images on a transparent screen of the future.

program, the reconciliation of Anderton and his wife, and a peaceful new life for the pre-cogs.

The portrayal of society five decades from now was a visual display of the best speculative thinking the production team could round up. Various people were hired to contribute to a seminar that Spielberg conducted in Santa Monica prior to production. Douglas Coupland, the novelist who coined the term "Generation X," was perhaps the most recognizable participant in the group. John Underkoffler of MIT Media Lab drew attention with his gesture technology. This was represented in the film when Anderton stood in front of a transparent screen, donned gloves with reflective beads and infared cameras. By pointing and gesturing with his hands at the screen, he moved images back and forth, off and on center, and zoomed them in and out. After watching the film, Pamela Barry, an engineer at Raytheon, has started to work on adapting this technology for military use in the real world (Karp).

Because the film is grounded in such realism, the story actually exposes more than other digital apocalyptic films. The clearest example is the depiction of a society under surveillance. It is common in science fiction to represent a government that watches its citizens around the clock for purposes of control, such as in George Orwell's *1984*. In this film, it is the marketers who conduct such close 24-hour scrutiny in order to launch direct sales pitches at each and every moment. Of course the mechanism is appropriated by government officials in their pursuit of the protagonist during the center part of the movie. This close scrutiny of the public in a consumer-driven society has already become a feature of advanced nations' landscapes in the 1980s and 1990s, primarily due to the introduction of scanned checkout at global supermarkets.[28] People habituated to machine scans have evolved even further into groups of passive consumers unable to assert their rights to privacy against either marketers or the police. Spielberg's conflation of market and government surveillances becomes a stronger representation of the current repression of people than is *The Matrix* or other contemporary films.

The wisdom of the storytellers is borne out in the most nightmarish scene of the movie, when the police use little mechanical crawlers nicknamed "spiders" to check out the occupants of a run-down apartment building as they conduct their manhunt. The moviemakers photograph the gamut of intrusions, from sexual to familial to scatological, and yet only one worn-out mother manages to utter even an ineffective protest as the police barge past her. She exclaims that they are terrifying her child. In a scene that seems to be straight out of Iraq, the cop replies to the mother with a belligerent, "If you don't want your kids to know terror, keep them away from me."

A specific Iraq reference would be premature. The United States did not invade that hapless country until nine months after the movie had been in theaters. But it fitted the atmosphere that preceded the invasion. The mood of the country and the world was already souring before September 11. Critics from around the world saw the movie's discourse about civil liberties as a reference to the recently passed PATRIOT Act, which undermined many of the Vietnam-era safeguards against overly zealous police action. The script proved to be wiser than its authors might have known, precisely because their artistic instincts about society extrapolated to imagine a citizenry already too prone to give up their civil rights, even when there is nothing at stake. The Hollywood creative team anticipated the repression of the Bush years, catching a wave rather than creating one. The American desire to sacrifice liberty for the sake of safety had been evident for quite a while. It was made manifest in the draconian imprisonment campaign that by 2002 had locked up a larger absolute number of people than any other country, and a larger percentage of the population than any other industrialized nation; 0.7 percent of the population was behind bars in that year. The percentage increase was more than threefold over 1980 and had risen steadily through the 22-year period ("Adults on probation," 2005). Drug possession is the crime that has the strongest correlation with the prison rise. It is a nonviolent offense that is only a preemptive indicator of violent crime. Perhaps the war on drugs showed it was only a matter of time until the United States would apply preemption to its foreign affairs also.

Minority Report is one of the darkest Spielberg movies, and the rescue of Anderton from prison and his restoration to a free life is a very near thing. Nigel Morris and Jason Vest have suggested that the end of the movie is a tack-on, not true to the logic of the story. Vest notes that when Anderton is haloed and being placed in his containment unit, he is told by the jailer that in the prison "All dreams come true." This remark legitimizes a reading of the rest of the movie as Anderton's dream coming true (Morris, 327–28). Spielberg does not put much cinematic energy into the conversion of Anderton's ex-wife, or the mechanics of how she managed to get Anderton out of jail. But I feel this false ending is too bleak an interpretation—neither Spielberg nor much of his audience would share it. The old-school ethos of Spielberg's approach to storytelling is to avoid false endings and to find balance between engagement and consensus, concern and despair. Other movies such as *Syriana* (2005) may give way to hopelessness, but not *Minority Report*.

Kaminski (once again Spielberg's director of photography) used a dark palette for the look of the film that at times made references to *Dark City* (1998) and *The Matrix* (1999). Spielberg was happy to borrow the tone and the look, but he was too old to tickle youthful minds with the ontological teasers of those two movies. We should understand that his questioning of reality always remained grounded in realism. Critics hailed the accomplishment and the box office swung up to gross $335 million worldwide. *Minority Report* did well in Europe and very well in Far East Asia. In particular, the Asian markets responded to Tom Cruise and the future setting of the film.

Minority Report launches a cycle of Spielberg films that finally comes to an end with *Indiana Jones and the Kingdom of the Crystal Skull* in 2008. The cycle is a response to the crisis in democracy, with films ranging from the historic-realistic to ones that belong to the current genre of the digital apocalypse. Spielberg was now reaping the fruit of all his ventures into the past, particularly the thoughtful forays such as *Empire* and even *Amistad*. He was now willing to take his audience through a series of ambiguous stories that were considerably less assuring than the crowd-pleasers of previous decades. The visual style was also changing, since the director was less willing to dictate to the audience a particular set of emotions. Although moments in *Minority Report* dazzled the eye with the possibilities of vertical transportation and other technologies, there were few obvious point-of-view scenes. Instead, the movie kept asking the audience to reinterpret visual information and to decipher whose point of view was determining the story, as images from the pre-cog Agatha kept repeating on screen in different parts of the story.

Minority Report is also interesting because it is a hybrid of the historical and the technological future. It looks like other digital apocalypse films because of its setting in the year 2054, but the story directly addresses the contemporary American attitudes towards fear, surveillance, and justice. It does not have to forge a consensus view and is willing to become socially engaged. Spielberg has worked through the blockbuster style to finally achieve his ambition of historical imagination. The next chapter takes us through his subsequent films, which do not achieve *Minority Report*'s high point, although they continue a new spirit of serious reflection about the state of America and the world.

7

SPIELBERG AND DARK VISIONS

The next two Spielberg films, *Catch Me If You Can* and *The Terminal*, were publicized as light entertainment but the lightness of either was debatable. *Catch Me If You Can* was released in December 2002, six months after the triumph of *Minority Report*. Leonardo DiCaprio starred in a story about a real teenager named Frank Abagnale who actually went on a notorious spree by forging checks in the early 1960s. Spielberg read the script of *Catch Me* in 2000 when Leonardo DiCaprio had already decided to do the film. He did not commit until 2001, after various schedule conflicts forced other directors to step aside and Spielberg found a time that coincided with DiCaprio's availability. It was the first time he had worked with DiCaprio, whose star had been shining brightly since *Titanic* (1997). Tom Hanks and Christopher Walken also took key roles.

Spielberg jumpstarts the film with the theme of appearance trumping substance in a very early scene. Frank Abagnale, Senior (Christopher Walken), wakes up his teenage son Frank Junior (Leonardo DiCaprio) to get him to masquerade as his chauffeur on the very slim chance that this will impress the bank loan officer into extending him credit. But modern life is undercutting the Abagnales. Chase Manhattan Bank is too big to take notice of whether Frank Sr. is being chauffeured or not. When Frank confronts a Chase officer in order to get a loan, the man advises him to go to his local neighborhood bank where the officer will know him. Mr. Abagnale ineffectively complains that his own bank no longer exists, having been forced into bankruptcy precisely by the large Chase Manhattan Bank.

The lack of credit precipitates a crisis in the family, as the father loses his store to unpaid taxes. The family moves from a beautiful New Rochelle suburban ranch house to a walk-up apartment. Frank Jr.'s French mother Paula (Nathalie Baye) starts an adulterous affair that leads to a divorce and a remarriage to a more successful businessman who gives her a House Beautiful. Frank runs away from the divorce at the tender age of 16 to make his own way in the world. But the world is no longer a place where a 16-year-old can legitimately make his own way, even one as brilliant as Frank. Thus he engages in that most modern of activities: identity switching. This is before the internet, so he builds new identities the old-fashioned way, through the creation of false documents with scissors and glue. The underage Frank Junior assumes the identity of an airline pilot, a doctor, and a lawyer, while always writing bad checks. Carl Hanratty (Tom Hanks) is the FBI man who pursues him relentlessly and finally brings him to justice. Once Frank is in prison, Carl starts getting advice from him on how to detect fraudulent checks. In return Frank gets his sentence reduced in order to work at the FBI. The movie ends on a final note of mutual trust being established between the policeman and the con artist, the only successful relationship in the film.

This is the innocent world before the 1963 Kennedy assassination. Spielberg explained, "This was a very moral time. This was a safe time, relatively speaking in America; when someone like Frank Abagnale, based on charm, personality and presentation, could pull these scams. Frank has told me that you couldn't do this today, that today he could never do what he did all those years ago because the country's changed." Not only the country but also the audience has changed. Spielberg also states, "I compare lightness with movies I have seen years and years ago when lightness of touch was something that was pretty standard fare. It's a little harder to do today because there is more cynicism" (Spielberg and Scorsese, 23).

Previously, in December 2001, Steven Soderbergh had recycled *Ocean's Eleven* in an update that was also trying to recapture a lighter zeitgeist. The hit movie had featured a group of loveable casino thieves. The advance word claimed that *Catch Me* also recaptured the romance of flight and the optimistic Technicolor atmosphere of the early sixties. But the movie's tone was surprisingly more in tune with the post-2001 malaise. Its script was permeated by new-millennium anxieties such as wayward parents, downward mobility, growth of corporations, and identity switching. The concept of "cool" in *Catch Me* becomes a brittle attempt to romanticize a world that trusted appearance more than achievement. Only one sequence set in sun-drenched Florida really had the bright shiny surfaces of the Space Age. Otherwise the scenes consisted of gloomy darkened hotel-room sets, autumnal and wintery New Rochelle exteriors and rainy locations in Georgia and Louisiana. Frank was finally cornered in a grimy industrial printing plant in France and thrown into a dungeonlike prison. Spielberg has little desire to brighten the story and the acting by DiCaprio, Hanks, and Walken is similarly somber and psychological rather than comic and light.

Spielberg seemed to have caught the serious bug and could not bring himself to portray a light-hearted America.

And yet he was pulling his punches. At every step in *Catch Me If You Can* the chicanery suggested something more rotten at the core than the film wanted to confront. The film emphasized the father-son relationship as one of real admiration. In addition the government agent plays by the book, and is incorruptible if also priggish and sour. This may be the FBI of J. Edgar Hoover but there are no illegal wiretaps, no hints of perversity or lack of respect for nonconformists. There is no xenophobia when the G-men interview Mrs. Abagnale. Spielberg indulged a longing for a time when the movies could still portray upright, trustworthy men and women who worked for the government.

Todd McCarthy's review in *Variety* complained about the evenhandedness. Even Martin Scorsese commented on his colleague's refusal to embrace current cynicism in an attempt to hold on to older values. The critics were mixed, unable to interpret whether the movie was a social condemnation or not. Some treated it as a light romp and appreciated the break from the streak of serious Spielberg films. The *New York Times* was taken in by the window dressing when Stephen Holden wrote, "The game-show excerpt, which follows a cool-handed animation title sequence, sets the lighthearted tone of a movie that admires Frank almost to the point of suspending moral judgment." Many were turned off by the disconnection between the tone and the promised atmosphere. A Boston newspaper decided it was not so light-hearted and then complained that Spielberg did not have the artistic genius to be so serious (Verniere).

The film was an international hit (worldwide $351 million box office). It did particularly well in Great Britain (despite critical pans), driven by the star power of DiCaprio (Groves). Its earnings were appreciably higher than DiCaprio's other

Even in the not-so-sunny 1960s, the Abagnales (father and son) are trapped by corporate America.

film of the moment, the bloody *Gangs of New York* (2003). Leo's fans obviously picked Spielberg's work in order to see the young star in a role that was a better fit for his skills and appearance. A comparable film that also featured a young imposter in the 1950s/1960s era—*The Talented Mr. Ripley* (1999)—was much more sexualized and violent than *Catch Me* and earned less than half the box office. On the other hand *Catch Me* did only two-thirds the business of *Ocean's Eleven*. In order to put together its audience the publicity department was correct to promote lightness. But Spielberg restrained himself from the lightness of outright wish fulfillment by following the real-life story of Frank Abagnale.

The duality of the film followed the apprehensive tone of *Minority Report*. In discussions with students I have discovered that many watched these two films without even realizing that Spielberg had directed them. While I doubt this was widespread, it does support a feeling that the filmmaker was using the not-so-distant past and the speculative future to engage the contemporary darkness. But too many, including the filmmaker himself, expected 1960s nostalgic innocence for Spielberg to realistically portray the tragedy of the Abagnale story. In the next film Spielberg retreats even further into audience expectations of a story that redeems America.

GENEROUS FABLE: *THE TERMINAL*

In this film Spielberg uses a complete fiction to tell the audience that America's multicultural society is still capable of Capraesque generosity. In today's JFK airport, Victor Navorski (Tom Hanks), a visitor from the fictional Krakozhia, is going through customs. He is refused entry because Krakozhia fell apart in a revolution during his flight and there is no home government that can validate his passport. He cannot be sent back, either. He is confined to the airport's international lounge by the US customs official Frank Dixon (Stanley Tucci). While trapped, the foreigner actually settles down to learn English and to survive through various tricks in the international lounge. It is not too hard, since he is surrounded by the boutique outlets of the great food and clothing chains of America. He shows skill at construction, and gets an under-the-table job with an airport contractor. He becomes friends with airport workers who are themselves marginalized by race and immigrant status from mainstream America, and pursues a romance with an airline stewardess, Amelia Warden (Catherine Zeta-Jones), who has suffered her own marginalization by getting involved with a married man. Ultimately the friends, the various customs agents, and the entire airport staff conspire to thwart Dixon and to let Navorski into the country to fulfill the mission of visiting a jazz player who was once beloved by Navorski's father. His romance does not work out, but he returns to Krakozhia with his mission accomplished.

The Terminal is not a biopic although it is inspired by the true story of Mehran Karimi Nasseri, an Iranian who lived in Charles DeGaulle Airport in Paris from 1988 to 2006.[29] The fictional problem in The Terminal does not bear much historical scrutiny. The story is premised on a fictional country with a fictional language and evokes other earlier movie-invented countries, such as Fredonia, Grand Fenwick, and others (almost always vaguely middle-European). Tom Hanks's Victor Navorski owes an unworldly patience to Andy Kaufman's Latka Gravas from the TV show Taxi (ABC 1978–1982). Hanks engages in a physical comedy that Spielberg and Kaminski capture in sweeping camera movements that even pivot 360 degrees to let the movement flow. The movement here presents the character to the viewer as he engages his situation; it is not visceral or thrill-seeking.

Spielberg gave his international audience a better view of the US than the Bush government deserved. The film was released on June 9, 2004, fifteen months after the United States invaded Iraq. By this time the United States was fully committed to unilateralism and a refusal to respect its alliances and its relationships with the rest of the world. The illegal detention camps at Guantanamo started receiving prisoners on January 11, 2002, marking the first time the United States government openly imprisoned people without a legal scheme by which to process them. Throughout these years following the attack of 2001, the United States implemented a series of border-crossing proceedings that were arbitrary and onerous.

Jeff Nathanson was brought in to rewrite the script and his publicity material refers obliquely to this political background. He says "this story allows us, in a very entertaining way, to explore some issues that I think are paramount to everything that's going in our country right now" (Dream-Works). What does he mean by "everything that's going in our country right now"? That becomes the question that guides the individual reaction to the film. Is it a depiction of a government that no longer obeys its own rules? Is it a depiction of a country that cannot come to an agreement about an immigration policy and cannot decide what to do about the twelve or more millions who are already here illegally? Or is it a celebration of the humanity of people who can still overcome the barriers? *The Terminal* becomes another open text in Spielberg's new century.

This openness to interpretation leads to some overseas expressions of frustration. A Thai newspaper, *The Nation*, complained that this movie once again shows that Spielberg "lacks backbone, immediately apologising for past works the minute a moral crusader knocks on his door." Perhaps a more targeted arrow was launched from Malaysia. "It is a far cry from the post Sept. 11 reality when we have to take off our shoes and unload all our bags for inspection at all airports in the US" (Moh). Cosmo Landesman of *The Sunday Times London* castigates the movie for not being the *Catch-22* of the age of globalization. "There's the potential here for a chilling critique of American bureaucracy or a light measured romance in the vein of '*Lost in Translation*.' Ultimately it straddles both and achieves neither" (Calhoun).

Frank Dixon may be the first exception to Spielberg's usual sympathetic portrayal of government figures, but he is not a loose cannon. He plays by the rules, despite his mean instincts. Indeed Navorski counter-traps him by obeying the rules. Dixon doesn't want Navorski to remain in the international lounge and he will not try to get a legitimate State Department clearance for the foreigner. Instead he tries to tempt Navorski into becoming an illegal intruder into the US, or alternately into falsely claiming refugee status. The audience cannot quite read Navorski's refusal to fall into these traps. Is he naïve or is he wise? The naïvete of Navorski resonates with the famous World War One-era Czech character of the good soldier Schweik. Navorski slowly gained the confidence of the shopkeepers and maintenance workers, particularly after he had solved a Russian transient's dilemma. The film shows him forming a close bond with a troika that included a Hispanic, a Hindu, and an African American, and they in turn facilitate his romance and his entry into the country. Spielberg's re-representing of the community spirit, however, exposes how vanished that spirit was in 2004 America.

The duality of Spielberg's impulses opens up our understanding of the airport as a space. The entire airport set was built for the movie in the desert near Palmdale, California. Some of the construction costs were offset when the various American corporations built mock-ups of their airport booths at their own expense. The corporations included Citigroup,

The airport set of The Terminal *was built to represent much of the consumer large chain stores.*

Verizon, American Express, Hudson News, Burger King (but no McDonalds), and the list goes on. Does the camera mock these boutiques and the antiseptic life of the airport, or does it promote them in a shiny environment that easily is more attractive than any real airport? It is the same question that came up when he portrayed the suburbs in *Close Encounters* and *E.T.*, and when the camera surveyed diegetic Jurassic merchandise in the movie that was already in real-life retail stores. In all of these movies Spielberg's visual language simultaneously condemns and takes pleasure in the sensual images of consumerism. But as we saw with *Jurassic Park*, the audience can be baffled by the ambiguity of marketing within the film.

The three films—*Minority Report, Catch Me,* and *The Terminal*—represent a trajectory circling back towards Spielberg's instinctual faith in the American people and feel-good finessing of conflicts. But the audience dwindled as the trajectory continued. *The Terminal* did not satisfy a desire shared by critics, parts of the audience, and the filmmaker for a serious engagement with heightened stakes in a world frightened by terrorism and increasingly uneasy about the unlimited expansion of marketplace values.

The negative costs for the movie hovered around the MPAA average for major motion pictures that year ($62.4 million) and its box office was above average (worldwide $290 million). But DreamWorks was only a mini-major and wanted really big hits. The film could be considered a disappointment, since it earned less than the recent averages for either Spielberg or Hanks and DreamWorks executives started to think of selling off parts of the company. Spielberg was now at a crossroads with his career and announced plans for several movies, betraying hesitancy about his relationship with his audience. He was covering his bets when he expressed interest in the fourth installment of Indiana Jones, which was sure to become a revenue-generating event. He also announced *War of the Worlds* with Tom Cruise. Here the motivation was more interesting. It was a blockbuster film that would be following the success of *Independence Day* (1996). But it would also be the definitive Spielberg use of 9/11 attack images designed to attract a blockbuster audience. Spielberg felt that his audience was also interested in the *issues* of the post-9/11 world and not just its *images*, so he announced a third project. This was about the systematic hunting of the 1972 Palestinian terrorists who had plotted to murder Israeli athletes at the Munich Olympics. This was a counter-movement from his other projects, since Spielberg was asking himself and his audience to forego filmic complacency.

THE TURN TOWARDS THE DIGITAL APOCALYPSE

Even as the hard-bodied hero faded in the last decade, there had been a rise of end-of-the-world scenarios on television and film that featured digital effects. In 1993, Fox TV launched the very influential show *The X-Files* (Fox, 1993–2002). This weekly series told stories of the paranormal and aliens while administering heavy dosages of paranoia. It brought hints of the digital apocalypse into US living rooms every Sunday evening. Its tone influenced several 1995 releases ranging from *Virtuosity* and *Johnny Mnemonic* to *Strange Days*. In 1996 Sony released the Playstation console, propelling the computer-game business to a new level of cultural prominence. The cycle of games turned more towards apocalyptic role players as the image, movement, and space became more realistic.

The digital image could easily present higher levels of destruction and mayhem than celluloid photography, no matter how tricky. If only for this reason it was natural that the content of the movies turn towards larger-scale disasters than in the seventies. In the seventies an anonymous skyscraper could catch fire, a city could be shaken by an earthquake, or an ocean liner could turn upside down. But the spectacular events were shown in short takes. Now the White House blows up; the entire world succumbs to crippling changes in the environment, and the largest ship in the world cracks in two as it sinks into the Arctic Ocean, thrusting the audience into the experience for extended periods of time. Digital has become both the technique and the subject matter.

This larger scale of filmic digital destruction matches the spirit of the times. The end of the Cold War might have lessened fears of nuclear warfare. Instead the world has fragmented into dangerous factions, some with great capacities for hostility and destruction. The macro fragments of nations and groups have been mirrored on the micro level. In everyday life, people do not form bonds through proximity. The Walkman and subsequently the cell phone and the iPod keep people separate from others within the same space. It is a fully atomized world where few acknowledge their fellow passengers.

In this fragmented world, stories of overwhelming destruction will create the compensatory fiction of people coming together to share an experience. For example, what if, in the midst of this street where no one looks at another, a bomb goes off; a comet hits; a Tyrannosaurus rex snatches a human being? Would not everyone look up together from their Walkmans and iPods and pay attention to the threat? Storytellers of our times imagine and represent the restored collective people reacting to large-scale acts of violence. The representations of these awesome acts of violence also bring the audience together in the theater to watch the movies. In the current world of the imagination it is easy to see why the current cycle of apocalyptic filmmaking arose to take advantage of the new technology to tell stories about our new anxieties.

The strange year of 2004 revealed new movie audience formations along political lines with the combined releases of Gibson's *Passion of the Christ* and Moore's *Fahrenheit 911*. *Passion of the Christ* might have merely revived the ecumenical audiences for the 1950s religious epic movies (for instance, *Ben Hur, The Greatest Story Ever Told*), but Gibson insisted on presenting the final week of Jesus' life on earth with medieval and mystical overlays that facilitated a divisive and extreme interpretation. He borrowed the visceral style of the blockbuster and used the camera to plunge the viewers into hypervisual displays of Jesus' punishment. His blood flies onto the lens (and the viewer) as he is whipped in close-up. This was the direct influence of the Omaha Beach scene from *Saving Private Ryan*. Despite the blockbuster style, no major Hollywood distributor picked up the film. Gibson went outside for financing and the independent studio Newmarket Films distributed *Passion*. They used the unusual strategy of marketing to evangelical and other conservative Christian groups. The film did extremely well with the wide audience, despite its extreme controversial tone (many thoughtful commentators accused the film of anti-Semitism).

Michael Moore also made a film that polarized audiences. *Fahrenheit 911* used footage of the Bush administration to visually illustrate Moore's narration, which charged the leadership with apathy towards early warnings of terrorist attacks and demagoguery after the attacks. It drew hostile criticism from media pundits, administrative spokespeople, and politicians, yet earned the highest box office receipts of any documentary film to date. The producers (the Weinstein brothers) had to go outside of Hollywood to get a Canadian distributor, Lions Gate, when the Walt Disney Company reneged on its promise to handle the film, obviously for reasons of political timidity. The two films together suggested that for the moment, audiences were attracted to ideologically driven films instead of the usual Hollywood consensus mode.

SPIELBERG'S CONFLICT: *WAR OF THE WORLDS* AND *MUNICH*

Spielberg always had an instinct for the broad mainstream of consensus. Perhaps the pulled punches of *Catch Me* and the fantasy of *The Terminal* were symptoms of a broad mainstream that was evaporating very quickly. He had been working away from the jingoism of the Reagan era, but he was still a man who supported the "global war on terror." Many Americans, including liberals and including Spielberg, supported the invasion of Iraq, although his subsequent strong support of the Democrats during the 2004 presidential race showed that he, along with many others, had come to regret his position. It is evident that his next two films, *War of the Worlds* and *Munich*, are inadvertent testimonies to the conflicts within a liberal mind regarding the mood of fear and vengeance that swept the United States after the 2001 terrorist attack. As such they drew different-sized audiences.

ATOMIZED POPCORN: *WAR OF THE WORLDS*

War of the Worlds was the first one of the pair to be released in the summer of 2005. It was done quickly, with an unprecedented amount of digital imagery, put together on an abbreviated production schedule. One might view this release (and the subsequent *Indiana Jones and the Kingdom of the Crystal Skull*, 2008) as Spielberg going back to popcorn mode in order to renew his power in the industry. It was directly based on H. G. Wells's novel.[30] Aliens invade the earth and start destroy-

ing human life without mercy and without regard. The protagonist is a self-centered man named Ray Ferrier (Tom
Cruise) whose marriage has derailed. He is a blue-collar union
man living in New Jersey. His ex-wife and her new upwardly
mobile professional husband show up to leave Ray's two children with him for the weekend. The story is about the self-
involved man who has to learn to care for someone else.
When the aliens emerge from the ground to invade the earth,
he has no more understanding of what is happening than
anyone else. Ray is not Roy Neary of *Close Encounters*.

The aliens are not from Spielberg's previous science fiction
either. They are neither elongated smooth beings nor cuddly
extra-terrestrials, but are now oversized reptiles, operating
huge killing machines from atop giant moving tripods. Ray
manages to jumpstart a truck and starts driving to reunite the
children with their mother in Boston. The invasion is everywhere and no humans seem to be able to band together to
survive or to oppose the aliens. This is a striking contrast with
the 1955 movie version of the H. G. Wells novel, in which
people get together to fight (Gordon). Even *Independence Day*
featured cooperative teamwork. But in 2005 Spielberg envi-
sions people exchanging gunfire with each other in order to
commandeer cars. Ferrier actually kills Harlan Ogilvy (Tim
Robbins), a man who takes him and his daughter (Dakota
Fanning) into his cellar for safety, merely because he suspects
Ogilvy will expose them with his plan for resistance. There
is a brief glimmer of solidarity when Ferrier's son (Justin
Chatwin) runs off to join the soldiers, rebuking his father's
concern for self.

As in every retelling of *War of the Worlds*, the aliens are
finally stopped by an earthly virus. Ferrier reaches a devastated
Boston with his daughter and improbably reunites with his
ex-wife, her husband and family, and even his son. Spielberg
visually quotes the ending of John Ford's *The Searchers* (1956)

when he shows Ferrier saving his family and yet unable to join them inside his ex-wife's parents' home. But the older movie had good reason to exclude the hero (named Ethan Edwards and played by John Wayne) from the community at the end. Edward's primitive set of values had barely been suppressed in his act of mercy towards his niece and he had no place in a settled community. In contrast, *War of the Worlds* does not question Ray Ferrier's actions and his lack of communal solidarity, because no one in the film, except the crazy Ogilvy, proposes working together. Spielberg's ending misquotes Ford's Hollywood. It is an ending that the audience accepted and Spielberg uses it to reflect audience ambivalence rather than shape it. Indeed, the extreme right-wing TV commentator Bill O'Reilly praised the film as reflecting the view of everyday Americans rather than a few Beverly Hills pinheads (Hoberman). One hopes the filmmaker, who was already engaged in directing *Munich*, winced at such praise.

NEITHER TRUE NOR FALSE: *MUNICH*

Munich is Spielberg's most overt embrace of ambiguity. It is destined to be so since it is neither fictional nor factual. It is based on true events that cannot be known because they remain state secrets. Therefore the movie uses different modes to present the set of events that are public, and those that are necessarily fictional, or at least speculative. The public events are the brutal seizure and subsequent murders of the Israeli athletes during the 1972 Summer Olympics in Munich, Germany. The fictional ones are the actions of avenging Israeli agent Avner and his team. There is even a hybrid between the two worlds: the re-imaginings by Avner of the experiences of the Israeli athletes in the hours before their killings. The movie relies heavily on re-imaginings and reaction shots, but less and less can these shots tell the audience how to react.

The film begins in linear cinematic mode as the Palestinians scale the fence and force their way into the Israeli dormitory. Then it switches to television coverage of the event, using real TV footage but never presenting these images to the audience directly. Instead there is always a mediating diegetic audience of Israeli citizens, Palestinian refugees, various political leaders, and finally the main character Avner and his wife Daphna (Ayelet Zurer). The secondhand nature of the television images (which the director can expect older members of his audience to remember) is the opposite of immersion. It asks the audience to reflect on how these images are being used by the news industry as well as the terrorists to send different messages to different audiences. After this opening section, the film comes back to the massacre of the Israeli athletes—not through TV video, but through the interior flashbacks of Avner. It is a double fiction, since Avner was not a witness to the actual events.

Munich *features fictional characters watching real events on television. It is the most mediated of Spielberg's films.*

The film enters into full fictional mode as the camera records a staging of the Israeli cabinet deciding to hunt down and kill various figures associated with Palestinian terrorism. Avner is recruited to lead a five-man team and he has to leave home before his pregnant wife gives birth. Since the team is instructed not to use official Israeli intelligence, they start purchasing information from a shadowy nonaligned family who facilitate all sorts of illegal activities from their countryside retreat in France. At one point Louis (Mathieu Amalric), the son of the facilitating family, is suspicious that Avner has betrayed their trust. But Avner re-establishes it when the patriarch Papa (Michael Lonsdale) approves of Avner as a family man, not a government bureaucrat.

The team kills some of their targets and is frustrated reaching other targets. Meanwhile, they learn from television of an outside world where the cycle of terrorism and revenge continues unabated. In their netherworld they meet and debate their enemy—the Palestinian terrorists—without revealing their own identity. The debate is the one opportunity that Spielberg and the scriptwriter Tony Kushner give to the Palestinian cause to voice its grievance, but in the context of the story it is somewhat artificial. As the team itself is hunted down and loses several of its members, Avner grows increasingly desperate that nothing is being accomplished. His official Israeli liaison Ephraim (Geoffrey Rush) tries to debrief him, but Avner refuses to reveal his own sources and flees to Brooklyn, New York. Ephraim makes one further attempt at a meeting with Avner on the banks of New York's East River. As the two cannot come to an agreement, the camera pulls away to pan the Manhattan skyline to find the intact World Trade Center towers off on the horizon (as they would have been in 1973). Their meaning as the final image of the film is uncertain, however, since Americans cannot make any more sense out of terrorism than can Avner.

There is not a glimmer of wish fulfillment. The story is not quite an official tragedy, since the main character survives, but Avner has been damaged by his experience. He cannot escape his demons, and even visualizes murders as he makes love to his wife. On the other hand, the story does not veer into nihilism. Spielberg constantly allows the characters to question the demands of justice and the motives of governments. They want a positive belief in civilized justice. Maybe it was this positivism that attracted the strong negative reaction from commentators such as David Brooks of the *New York Times*, Charles Krauthammer of the *Washington Post*, and Leon Wieseltier of *The New Republic*. These neo-cons could not accept that Israelis would or should wring their hands over taking vengeance. They condemned the film. In another perspective, Joseph Massad writes that *Munich* "does not deviate much from Zionist propaganda, which has always claimed that Jewish soldiers 'shoot and cry.'"

The vitriol was more bitter than anticipated. Spielberg felt compelled to articulate his position more clearly after the film's release by adding an extended introduction to the DVD version, which reached the market in March 2006. Tony Kushner made outspoken remarks in defense of the script, while Spielberg's comments were remarkably in the spirit of a philosopher of history. He limited the responsibility of the filmmaker by denying that his films gave answers. The stated goal of *Munich* was merely to raise questions through the power of fictional storytelling. He stated that this was not a documentary. More to the point, he justified the script's empathy for all of its characters. This was done in order to understand, not to justify their actions, he said.

DVD sales were relatively high (Arnold), which shows an engaged adult audience since a DVD purchase suggests a stronger interest in the film than a rental or a theater ticket purchase. *Munich* was strong in other secondary markets.

Foreign earnings were respectable, with $131 million worth of tickets being sold. It was only the US box office that was disappointing at $47 million. Was it that *Munich* was a story foreign to the US? But its theme of vengeance against terrorists is distinctly rooted in the present American experience. Comparatively, *Munich* did almost as well as *Syriana* and better than *Good Night and Good Luck*. It garnered 5 Academy Award nominations (and did not win any). Spielberg, again, had been able to command attention for an issue because of his status as the leading American filmmaker.

As of this writing, *Munich* is the last attempt by the father of the blockbuster to engage the history of our times. The cycle has wound down.[31] The American audience seems to be tiring of engagement, after their surprising interest in 2004's *Fahrenheit 911* and *Passion*. One non-American critic summarizing the lack of box office support for the crop of 2005 serious films wrote, "Obviously, the general American population is not as caught up with thought-provoking cinema as the critics are" (Chin). It could have been that quite a few films were released on serious matters, and this diluted interest in any single title. It could also be that by 2006 the unpopular Iraq involvement continued; only the 2008 Presidential campaign relieved a certain passivity that had set in after George W. Bush's re-election. As the Obama campaign started to become possible, Spielberg had not identified where he wanted to go with historical engagement. He pushed back on his plan to make a film about Abraham Lincoln during the Civil War. Instead he turned to recycling his career with Indiana Jones, and planned a future project based on the Belgian comic-book hero Tintin, who has a retrospective "action" quality resembling that of Indiana Jones.

Indiana Jones and the Kingdom of the Crystal Skull (Indy IV) is Spielberg's renewal of relationships with his audiences, a more international one than when the first Raiders came out.

The Spielberg/Lucas revival relied heavily on the built-in global recognition factor of Indiana Jones and the great desire of foreign audiences to see the old stars, particularly Harrison Ford.

The setting is the 1950s, and Professor Jones is several decades older than when we last saw him on the eve of World War Two. Now the Soviets are the enemy and they have him in custody. They use him to capture an alien crystal skull from a US military warehouse. His adversary is an intelligent Soviet agent, Col. Dr. Spalko (Cate Blanchett). He escapes both the Soviets and a nuclear blast by hiding inside a refrigerator. Jones is subjected to an interview with the FBI which turns hostile when they imply his former colleague has communist connections. A motorcyclist, Mutt Williams (played to the hilt as a greasy juvenile delinquent by Shia LeBeouf), brings Jones a tip about crystal skulls in the Amazon and together they take off to find the skulls. The Soviets, however, are hot on the same pursuit and their paths intersect. Along the way Jones discovers that Mutt Williams and his mother, Jones's former girlfriend Marion Ravenswood (Karen Allen), are involved in the caper. There are various escapes, kidnappings, and fights until the mystery is revealed and the good guys prevail. The final act is the marriage of Indiana Jones and Marion Ravenswood.

All the styles that the audience already knew from the previous Indy Jones movies are used purposefully. The camera work is mobile and immersive. The final chase goes further than the three-pronged chase of *The Last Crusade*, setting up four prongs by paralleling two pairs of good guys and bad guys chasing at high speeds along a clifftop. Nonetheless, the editing is surprisingly linear, without the intricate foreshadowing that Buckland analyzes in *Raiders of the Lost Ark*. There is a new willingness on Spielberg's part to stop topping himself and other blockbuster directors with spectacle and breathless excitement. He compares himself in interviews to the makers of *The Bourne Ultimatum* (2007) and admits that he would not and could not use such a frenetic editing pace, although he admires Paul Greengrass's style.

The fourth installment of Indiana Jones fits in with other revivals of 1980s franchises such as Batman, Superman, Rambo, Rocky, and John T. McClane in the *Die Hard* series. The last three franchises had their final hurrahs at this time. *Live Free or Die Hard* (2007) had global box office revenues of $383 million, less than half of *Kingdom of the Crystal Skull*'s $780 million. The Sylvester Stallone movies both received under $200 million. The hard body had lost its universal appeal in a world that had come to resent American unilateralism. However, the two superhero movies, *The Dark Knight* (Batman) and *Superman Returns* (2006) did very well, with *The Dark Knight* surpassing *Kingdom of the Crystal Skull*. While the fading hard-bodied hero continued to act secure in his righteousness, Batman, Spiderman, Superman, the X-Men (and women) had all come to be conflicted and unsure of their missions. Their Hamlet-like doubt seemed to broaden their global appeal.

The Dark Knight, for example, is an extended narrative about the difference between a vigilante and the agents of the law. While the law as embodied by Harvey Dent (Aaron Eckhart) is subject to corruption, even Batman acknowledges that Harvey Dent is the greater man, and his reputation after death must be preserved. The film affirms the law as the final repository of the people's trust in society. It addresses the vigilante question directly. Spielberg, in contrast, has discreetly ignored hard-body nihilism, rejecting it for his own action stories although hints of its ideology permeate *War of the Worlds*. In 2008 Indiana Jones finds himself in a middling position between the conflicted comic-book heroes and the hard-bodied "armies of one."

CODA: OPEN QUESTIONS

Spielberg brought his global audience to the end of his political cycle with *Munich*. Although he and Lucas were hip enough to make reference to the anti-communist witch hunts of the 1950s, there were few socio-political issues in "Indy IV," nor are there such in Spielberg's near-term horizon. In addition, his dominance of the world's popular culture will ebb naturally as he slows down and as America takes a new path after the international global economic meltdown.

Nonetheless, there cannot be a conclusion to a book entitled *Steven Spielberg's America*. The meanings of Spielberg's body of work will continue to be particularly fluid because he was so successful at intervening in the mainstream at three different points in three different decades. I am most interested in his recent attempt at intervention during the current age of polarized politics. It was an attempt supported by an international audience; indeed, more strongly supported by foreigners than by his fellow Americans. This intervention, however, embedded in the cycle of films from *Saving Private*

Ryan to *Munich*, was heavily determined by the American perspective and by the original compact that the young Spielberg made with his domestic fans in order to launch his career.

Because he made this compact with the general American audience, there are omissions or indulgences in wish fulfillment about the troubled episodes of American history. Spielberg broke away from New Hollywood by turning the page on the legacy of Vietnam and the more difficult questions of the civil rights movement. His handling of race relations, even as late as *Amistad*, tiptoes around the sensibilities of both black and white Americans. These lacunae are the systemic weaknesses that disappear from view. In contrast, his wishful vision of an inclusive populist society achieved without public reform is a highly visible contradiction in his last cycle of films.

The contradiction is as simple as his identity as a transplanted East Coaster, trying to accommodate the ideology of individuals and free markets with liberal notions of fairness and equality. This describes Spielberg and it describes the state of the politically liberal imagination where alternative visions such as strong organized labor and socialism no longer make sense to a mainstream audience.

Spielberg's sunbelt values helped him ride the American cultural shift through the great Thermidorean reaction of the late 1970s and the next three decades. But when blockbuster Hollywood turned to bravado, Spielberg recycled the populist spirit of earlier American films. Therefore the contradiction between the value systems keeps popping up; it was successfully negotiated in *Minority Report*, where marketplace surveillance becomes preemptive government action and both the sunbelter and the liberal can disapprove. It is less negotiated and more apparent in the other films in the cycle.

Spielberg's sincere belief in his own goodness often justifies an over-the-top camera style that forces the viewer to respond rather than to interpret. But he has preserved the continuity of American popular culture, helping his audiences to seek positive political values from even the biggest budget movies.

Spielberg at the height of his career. His combination of sunbelt values and liberal populism has provided a distinct American perspective to the global audience.

APPENDIX

APPENDIX Releases, budget and box office figures for Spielberg movies.

USA RELEASE	TITLE	BUDGET $	DOMESTIC $000,000	FOREIGN $000,000	TOTAL $000,000	% Domestic
11/12/67	Duel	.75 mil		8.0	12.8	59
03/30/70	The Sugarland Express	2 mil	7.5	5.3	471.0	55
06/19/71	Jaws	11 mil	260.0	211.0	338.0	49
11/14/73	CE3K	20 mil	166.0	172.0	76.3	42
12/12/75	1941	31.5 mil	31.8	44.5	384.0	63
06/11/77	Raiders	22 mil	242.0	142.0	701.2	57
06/10/78	ET	10.5 mil	400.0	301.2	29.5	n/a
06/24/83	Twilight Zone	10 million	29.5	n/a	333.1	54
05/23/84	Temple of Doom	27 million	179.9	153.2	142.0	66
12/16/85	The Color Purple	15 million	94.0	48.0	65.8	34
12/09/87	Empire of the Sun	38 million	22.2	43.6	494.8	40
05/24/89	Last Crusade	37 million	197.2	297.6	77.3	57
12/22/89	Always	31 million	43.9	33.4	300.9	40
12/08/91	Hook	70 million	119.8	181.1		

12/09/93	*Jurassic Park*	65 million	357.0	563.0	920.0	39
11/30/93	*Schindler's List*	32 million	95.4	221.7	317.1	30
05/19/97	*Lost World*	73 million	229.0	386.0	615.0	37
12/04/97	*Amistad*	40 million	42.0	18.0	60.0	70
07/24/98	*Private Ryan*	70 million	217.0	268.0	485.0	45
12/26/01	*AI*	90 million	78.6	156.4	235.0	33
12/17/02	*Minority Report*	102 million	132.0	203.8	335.8	39
12/16/02	*Catch Me*	52 million	164.4	187.0	351.4	47
06/09/04	*Terminal*	60 million	78.0	141.0	219.0	36
06/23/05	*War of the Worlds*	132 million	234.0	357.0	591.0	40
12/24/05	*Munich*	70 million	47.0	131.0	178.0	26
05/22/08	*Crystal Skull*	185 million	317.0	470.0	787.0	40

various sources including Spielbergfilms.com, boxofficemojo.com and Shone.

NOTES

[1] Georg Lukacs has a similar powerful analysis of the function of the novel in his seminal work, *The Historical Novel*. Pierre Sorlin works with the philosophy of "presentism" in his work on historical films (208).

[2] "Road show" refers to a method of distributing films which would feature a lengthy heavily promoted performance in only a few big city premier movie theaters before moving on to other theaters in other cities.

[3] The huge success of *Brian's Song* (ABC 1971) showed the direction of the TV movie more clearly than *Duel*. The program format would evolve into melodramas based on topical human interest stories and attracting a largely female audience.

[4] See Jameson (27–30) for extended discussion of the class representations in *Jaws*.

[5] The screenplay for *American Graffiti* was inspired by Federico Fellini's *I Vitelloni* (1953).

[6] Peter Krämer insists that *Star Wars* is the all-age film that launches the blockbuster era, while Tom Schatz advocates for

the marketing innovations of *Jaws* as the beginning of the new epoch. I also accept the earlier film, which already had reunified audiences that had divided over road shows and New Hollywood.

[7] Note that Spielberg worked the opposite way to desexualize Hooper in order to pull in a younger audience while *Superman* began with the young audience and wanted to pull in the older viewers.

[8] Personal interview with Newman, December 1988.

[9] Yet when he himself became a top-money-earning director, his treatment of history in the *Back to the Future* series or in *Forrest Gump* (1994) was relatively unchallenging.

[10] See Buckland,136–43, for an extended analysis of the *Raiders* sequences.

[11] Lester Friedman makes an extensive argument against the charge that the Indiana Jones series was feeding the Reagan ideology (2006, 112–18). His defense, however, centers on the Indiana Jones character's development across the three films that were in existence in 2006. If we did not know the other films, it would be very difficult to defend the actions of Indiana Jones in the first film.

[12] Norman Rockwell painted many covers for the once-popular magazine *The Saturday Evening Post* and was inspired by his own New England surroundings. In the nineteenth century, the New England wooden frame house and side garden had spread throughout the country and had lost its regional specificity.

[13] The video game version of *E.T.* is considered one of the biggest flops in video game history.

[14] Although DeLaurentiis had already had several decades of fame and was soon destined to overreach when he tried to create his own studio in 1986.

[15] Colorado is a little too far north to really be part of the sunbelt, but its rapid development and its image as the New

West puts it in the same culture zone as Texas, Arizona, and California.

[16] In the twenty-first century, however, the international appeal of Will Smith and others has eroded the power of the cliché.

[17] Spielberg participated in restoring a version and provided commentary for the 2000 DVD release of *Lawrence of Arabia*.

[18] Jeffords also includes *Billy Jack* and *Walking Tall* in this cycle.

[19] *The Color Purple* was an obvious exception.

[20] Such as the US invasion of Panama in December 1989.

[21] George Lucas was more overtly interested than Steven Spielberg in the new technology and founded the Industrial Light and Magic Company to develop and sell special effects and computer technology to movie productions.

[22] Spielberg had found a new director of photography, Janusz Kaminski, who would become Spielberg's go-to D.P. for all subsequent movies. Later, in *Saving Private Ryan*, they would use a bleaching process to finesse the balance between black-and-white and color for a contemporary World War Two look. Interestingly, they would use that process again in *Minority Report*, which is set in the future.

[23] This is three million less than my estimate for *Empire of the Sun* and is the least seen Spielberg movie since *The Sugarland Express*.

[24] Friedman identifies *Cry Freedom* (1987) and *Glory* (1989) as two other mainstream movies that *Amistad* rebukes because of their infantile treatment of the nonwhite participants in the civil rights cause (272). I feel the contrast is strongest with *Mississippi Burning*, however, since it shares with *Amistad* an American legal setting.

[25] A typical Hollywood situation was that two other combat films reached the latter stages of development at Paramount

at the same time as *Private Ryan* but the Spielberg clout assured that his was the only one to go into production.

[26] Steven Spielberg avoids surveys of audiences and the other formal methods to identify pre-existing markets during pre-production.

[27] See my mention of Fredric Jameson's theory that science fiction is the new historical fiction in the Introduction.

[28] Steven's father Aaron Spielberg was one of the engineers who contributed to the technology of bar coding.

[29] The resemblance was close enough for DreamWorks to pay the Iranian $300,000 for his story rights. A closer examination of Nasseri's situation shows that his own recalcitrance led to his limbo status.

[30] *Independence Day* was done nine years earlier as a looser adaption of Wells's novel.

[31] Another sign of the completion of a cycle was the sale of DreamWorks to Paramount (a division of Viacom) at the time of the release of *Munich*. Spielberg no longer owned a big studio. This will hardly affect his autonomy as a filmmaker but it was a close of an interesting experiment in trying to create something new in the American film industry.

WORKS CITED

Adults on probation, in jail or prison, and on parole, United States 1980–2005. Table 6.1. (2005). Sourcebook of Criminal Justice Statistics Online. downloaded from http://www.albany.edu/sourcebook/wk1/t612005.wk1 on November 9, 2007.

American Film Institute. (1973, November 14). *Seminar with Steven Spielberg*. Los Angeles.

Arnold, T. K. (2006, May 18). "Munich" DVD tracks down 2 chart wins. *The Hollywood Reporter*. Downloaded from Lexus Nexus on July 21, 2007.

Barnes, B. (2008, July 27). A director's cut. *The New York Times*, Business Section, pp. 1, 6.

Baxter, J. (1996). *Steven Spielberg: The unauthorised biography*. London: HarperCollins.

Belton, J. (1992). *Widescreen cinema*. Cambridge, Mass.: Harvard University Press.

Benjamin, W. (1935/2005). Art in the Age of Mechanical Reproduction. In Meenakshi Gigi Durham and Douglas

Kellner (eds.) *Media and Cultural Studies* (pp. 48–70). Malden, Ma.: Blackwell Publishing.

Benson, S. (1987, Dec. 9). "Empire of the Sun" charts a boy's survival during war. *Los Angeles Times*, Section 6, p. 1.

Benzel, J. (1984, December). People's choice: Managing editor Pat Ryan. *Washington Journalism Review*, 6(10): 34–37.

Bernardoni, J. (1991). *The New Hollywood: What the movies did with the new freedoms of the seventies*. Jefferson, N.C.: McFarland & Co.

Blanchet, R. (2005). Deep impact: Emotion and performativity in contemporary blockbuster cinema. In Christian W. Thomsen and Angela Krewani (eds.), *Hollywood: Recent developments* (pp. 76–84). Stuttgart, Germany: Axel Menges Verlag.

Blum, D. (1986, March 24). Steven Spielberg and the dread Hollywood backlash. *New York*, 52–64.

Bobo, J. (1993). Reading through the text: The black woman as audience. In Manthia Diawara (ed.), *Black America cinema* (pp. 272–87). New York: Routledge.

Breskin, D. (1985, October 24). Steven Spielberg. *Rolling Stone* (459) 22–24, 70–76.

Buckland, W. (2006). *Directed by Steven Spielberg: Poetics of the contemporary Hollywood blockbuster*. New York: Continuum.

Busch, A. M. (1994, May 31). "Jurassic" is box office king, licensing prince. *The Hollywood Reporter*. Downloaded on June 7, 2007.

Caldwell, J. T. (1995). *Televisuality: Style, crisis, and authority in American television*. New Brunswick, N.J.: Rutgers University Press.

Calhoun, D. (2004, September 1). The terminal. *Time Out London*.

Champlin, C. (1986, February 2). Spielberg's escape from escapism. *Los Angeles Times*, pp. 12–18.

Chin, O. S. (2006, March 4). Hollywood reclaims its soul as politics returns to big screen. *The Straits Times* (Singapore). Downloaded from http://docs.newsbank.com on June 6, 2006.

Coontz, S. (1992). *The way we never were: American families and the nostalgia trap.* New York: Basic Books.

Coontz, S. (2006). Too close for comfort. *New York Times*, p. A21.

Corrigan, T. (1991). *A cinema without walls: Movies and culture after Vietnam.* New Brunswick, N.J.: Rutgers University Press.

DreamWorks. (2002). *The Terminal Press Kit.*

Eidsvik, C. (1988, Winter). Machines of the invisible: Changes in film technology in the age of video. *Film Quarterly* 42(2): 18–23.

Fleming, M. (1996, June 4). Spielberg, Hanks Hook; Par, Dreamworks may team for WWII pic "Ryan." *Daily Variety*, p. 1.

Foreign Flix making bid for Christmas cheer in U.S. (1991, Oct. 21). *Daily Variety.*

Freer, I. (2001). *The Complete Spielberg.* London: Virgin Publishing.

Friedman, L. D. (2006). *Citizen Spielberg.* Urbana: University of Illinois Press.

Gabler, N. (2001, September 16). This time, the scene was real. *The New York Times. Week in Review*, p. 2.

Geuens, J-P. (2000). *Film production theory.* Albany: State University of New York Press.

Goldfield, D. (2003, October). Searching for the sunbelt. *Magazine of History* 18(1): 3.

Gordon, A. M. (2008). *Empire of dreams: The science fiction and fantasy films of Steven Spielberg.* Lanham, Md.: Rowan and Littlefield.

Gormlie, F. (1992). Ballard's nightmares/Spielberg's dreams: Empire of the Sun. In J. Orr (ed.), *Cinema and fiction: New modes of adapting, 1950–1990*. Edinburgh: Edinburgh University Press.

Grindon, L. (1994). *Shadows on the past: Studies in the historical fiction film*. Philadelphia: Temple University Press.

Groves, D. (2003, February 10). O'Seas cools but "Catch Me" catches on. *Variety*, p. 20.

Hampton, H. (2003, January 12). Catch me if you can: French director Jean-Luc Godard is obsessed with running down his nemesis, Steven Spielberg. But the fleet-footed, crowd-pleasing American is outpacing him these days. *The Boston Globe*, p. D2.

Hansen, M. B. (2000). Schindler's list is not Shoah: The Second Commandment, popular modernism, and public memory. In Marcia Landy (ed.), *The historical film: History and memory in media* (pp. 201–17). New Brunswick, N.J.: Rutgers University Press.

Harrah, D. (1954, December). Aesthetics of the film: The Pudovkin-Arnheim-Eisenstein theory. *The Journal of Aesthetics and Art Criticism* 13(2): 163–74.

Hayes, D., & J. Bing. (2004). *Open wide: How Hollywood box office became a national obsession* (1st ed.). New York: Miramax Books/Hyperion.

Hedetoft, U. (2003). *The global turn: National encounters with the world*. Aalborg, Denmark: Aalborg University Press.

Hoberman, J. (2005, December 21). Jump cuts. *Village Voice*.

Holden, S. (2002, December 25). Film review: Taking to a gullible world like a mouse to Swiss cheese. *The New York Times*, Arts Section, p. 1.

Hollywood Foreign Press Association. (1993, December 9). Interview with Steven Spielberg.

Hollywood Foreign Press Association. (1993, December 10). Interview with Ben Kingsley and Ralph Fiennes.

Internet Movie Data Base (IMDB). http://www.imdb.com/ Sections/Genres/History/average-vote, Downloaded on June 10, 2007.

Jameson, F. (1992). *Signatures of the visible*. New York: Routledge.

Jarvis, J. (2003, March) Telephone interview with author.

Jeffords, S. (1994). *Hard bodies: Hollywood masculinity in the Reagan era*. New Brunswick, N.J.: Rutgers University Press.

Jordan, C. (2003). *Movies and the Reagan presidency: Success and ethics*. Westport, Conn.: Praeger.

Kael, P. (1974, March 18). The current cinema. *New Yorker*, 130–38.

Kael, P. (1976, November 8). The current cinema. *New Yorker*, 136–43.

Karp, J. (2005, April 12). Minority report inspires technology aimed at military. *Wall Street Journal*, pp. B1–B7.

Keane, S. (2006). *Disaster movies: The cinema of catastrophe*. New York: Wallflower Press.

King, G. (2002). *New Hollywood cinema: An introduction*. London: I. B. Tauris and Company.

Krämer, P. (2002). The best Disney film Disney never made. In Steve Neale (ed.), *Genre and contemporary Hollywood* (pp. 185–200). London: BFI Publishing.

Krämer, P. (2005). *The New Hollywood: From Bonnie And Clyde to Star Wars*. London, New York: Wallflower.

Landesman, C. (2004, September 5). Terminal limbo. *The Sunday Times London*.

Lev, P. (1993). *The Euro-American cinema*. Austin: University of Texas Press.

Lukacs, G. (1962). *The historical novel*. London: Merlin Press.

Mander, J. (1978). *Four arguments for the elimination of television*. New York: William Morrow and Company.

Massad, J. (2006, February 10). "Munich," or Palestinians making baklava: Spielberg's new film is emphatically about Israeli Jews and Israeli terrorism. *The Daily Star* (Beirut, Lebanon). Downloaded from http://docs.newsbank.com on June 6, 2006.

May, L. (2000). *The big tomorrow: Hollywood and the politics of the American way*. Chicago: University of Chicago Press.

McBride, J. (1997). *Steven Spielberg: A biography*. New York: Simon & Schuster.

McCarthy, T. (1982, June 16). "Independent" producers bruised as majors borrow their slants. *Daily Variety*, p. 22.

McCarthy, T. (2002, December 16). Catch Me If You Can. *Daily Variety*, p. 6.

Moh, L. C. (2004, October 23). Cast away at JFK Airport. *Malay Mail*.

Morris, N. (2007). *The Cinema of Steven Spielberg: Empire of Light*. London: Wallflower Press.

Mumford, L. (1961). *The city in history: Its origins, its transformations and its prospects*. New York: Harcourt, Brace and World.

Nadel, A. (1997). *Flatlining on the field of dreams: Cultural narratives in the films of President Reagan's America*. New Brunswick, N.J.: Rutgers University Press.

Nadel, A. (2005). *Television in Black-and-White America: Race and National Identity*. Lawrence, KS.: University Press of Kansas.

Nation, The (Thailand). (2004, September 9). Spielberg's worst blunder yet. *The Nation (Thailand)*.

Palmer, W. J. (1993). *The films of the eighties: A social history*. Carbondale: Southern Illinois University Press.

Pfeil, F. (1998). From pillar to postmodern: Race, class and gender in the male rampage film. In Jon Lewis (ed.), *The new American cinema* (pp. 146–86). Durham, N.C.: Duke University Press.

Riordan, P. M. (undated). He is legend: Richard Matheson. *Sci-Fi Station*. http://www.scifistation.com/matheson/matheson_index.html, downloaded on May 30, 2006.

Russell, J. (2007). *The historical epic and contemporary Hollywood: From Dances with Wolves to Gladiator*. New York: Continuum International Publishers.

Ryan, M., and Kellner, D. (1988). *Camera politica: The politics and ideology of contemporary Hollywood film*. Bloomington: Indiana University Press.

Sanello, F. (1996). *Spielberg: The man, the movies, the mythology*. Dallas, Tex.: Taylor Publishing.

Schickel, R. (1968). *The Disney version: The life, times, art and commerce of Walt Disney*. New York: Simon and Schuster.

Sheehan, H. (1992, July–August). Spielberg II. *Film Comment* 28: 66–71.

Shone, T. (2004). *Blockbuster: How Hollywood learned to stop worrying and love the summer*. New York: Free Press.

Sorlin, P. (1980). *The Film in history: Restaging the past*. Totowa, N.J.: Barnes and Noble.

Spielberg, S., and Scorsese, M. (2003, June). Catching movies with Steven Spielberg and Martin Scorsese. *DGA Magazine* 27(5): 22–28.

Steinberg, C. S. (1980). *Film facts*. New York: Facts on File.

Stempel, T. (2004). *American Audiences on movies and moviegoing*. Lexington, Ky.: University Press of Kentucky.

Tesson, C. (1998). L'amerique frontiere de l'absolu. *Cahiers du Cinema* 529: 61–65.

Verniere, J. (2002, December 25). Movie Review: Spielberg tries to be so hip it hurts. *The Boston Herald*, p. 33.

Wasser, F. (1995, February). Four-walling exhibition: Regional resistance to Hollywood. *Cinema Journal* 34(2): 51–65.

Wasser, F. (2001). *Veni, vidi, video: The Hollywood empire and the VCR*. Austin: University of Texas Press.

Wasser, F. (2002). Is Hollywood America? The transnation-
alization of the American film industry. In Steven Ross
(ed.), *Movies and American Society* (pp. 345–58). Malden,
Mass.: Blackwell Publishing.

Watts, S. (1997). *The Magic Kingdom: Walt Disney and the
American way of life.* New York: Houghton Mifflin.

Williams, R. (1974). *Television, technology and cultural form.*
Hanover, N.H.: Wesleyan University Press.

Wood, R. (1986). *Hollywood from Vietnam to Reagan.* New
York: Columbia University Press.

Wood, R. (1990). E.T. The Extra Terrestrial. In Nicholas
Thomas (ed.), *International dictionary of films and filmmakers. Vol. 1: Films* (pp. 293–95). London: St. James Press.

Wyatt, J. (1994). *High concept: Movies and marketing in Hollywood.* Austin: University of Texas Press.

INDEX